The last days of HMS Warspite in Cornwall 1947-1956

WARSPITE (above in foreground) with flags proudly flying at the July 1924 review of the fleet at Spithead by King George V. The ship is broadly as originally built before her first reconstruction. *Topfoto*

Sadly stranded on the rocks at Prussia Cove in 1947. *Author's collection*

The last days of HMS Warspite in Cornwall 1947-1956

www.worldshipsociety.org

ISBN: 978-1-9160589-7-2

Published in the United Kingdom by The World Ship Society Ltd,
Mayes House, Vansittart Estate, Arthur Road, Windsor, SL4 1SE,
United Kingdom

Page Layout by The Highlight Type Bureau Ltd, 29 Thorpe Lane, Leeds LS20 8LQ

Printed by Short Run Press Ltd, 25 Bittern Road, Exeter EX2 7LW

Front cover: **WARSPITE** seen ashore at Prussia Cove in May 1947. *Topfoto*

Dedicated to John Lennie MacQuarrie (1923-1950), pictured below, who died in an accident on board Warspite on 15 March 1950, to all who worked on Warspite in Cornwall and all who sailed on her in her distinguished career.

WARSPITE's motto – 'despise the hard knocks of war'

Prefaces

WARSPITE is a name I have been familiar with for over sixty years, in fact all my life. My father and his business partner were ever present during my childhood. In those early years I became used to the term “that was from the WARSPITE” as I spent many hours of my childhood wandering round the spacious yard at the Pool works of the East Pool Mine, Cornwall. It was there that my father and Neil Macdonald set up their MacSalvors business in 1957 after the WARSPITE project, the greatest salvage and dismantling operation in British waters, came to a close in 1956. Items of plant, equipment and materials were stored at the yard along with stock purchased from the MOD and the War Department (identified by their pusser’s arrow), as they developed their business in government surplus. It was a great pleasure for me when I joined MacSalvors and learned some of the skills employed on the WARSPITE such as oxyacetylene cutting, welding, dismantling and rigging and of course identifying the various types of scrap metals we encountered, important skills employed on the salvage operation. A number of years were to pass before I was able to gain a more personal connection with the WARSPITE wreck when I took up scuba diving. Diving in the shallows at Prussia Cove where the wreck ran aground and salvage began, I could collect various remnants from the wreck, marble tiles from the galley deck, a machinery plate bearing the ship’s name and small metal parts. Diving St Michael’s Mount, there are larger remnants, two boilers and keel steel submerged in the sand as well as many small artifacts ranging from cutlery to brass parts which have fallen progressively through the decks to the sea floor and their final resting place.

None of these experiences however hinted at the exhausting, tragic and ‘against the odds’ story of the salvage operation which took place at Prussia Cove and the subsequent dismantling operation which took a further six years to complete, leaving just a few tons of steel as a permanent marker to the resting place of the Grand Old Lady of the Royal Navy.

When I met Richard Holme, a distinguished maritime researcher, I was delighted to learn of his interest in the salvage story. Richard has a Masters degree in UK Shipbreaking history post 1945, within Newcastle University’s Marine Technology department. He is also editor of the Naval Dockyards Society newsletter and has already written a book on major shipbreaking centre, Cairnryan. He approaches his subject with careful consideration, a thorough examination of all the available facts and information, which is then scrupulously documented. He has produced here a riveting account which will be of interest to local residents, historians, sailors past and present and anyone who has an interest in a titanic struggle against the elements and the authorities. Richard’s against the odds narration brings the story to life some 70 years on in a well-researched and crafted account and a worthwhile publication.

Iain MacQuarrie, *Director, MacSalvors Ltd*

"A good read" is often said, but often unmerited. Not here: this is an extraordinary tale, told with exemplary skill; a history book that is carefully researched but is also a swashbuckling adventure story.

It's the tale of the demise of HMS WARSPITE, the battleship that had fought at Jutland, and at Crete, Matapan, Salerno, Normandy... the list is long and illustrious. She had received the most battle honours ever awarded to an individual ship in the Royal Navy. She was rightly nicknamed the 'Grand Old Lady'. Her motto was 'Bella dura despicio': 'Despise the hard knocks of War'. During her service career, WARSPITE had lived up to her motto, enduring shellfire, bombing, ramming, mines, and even a guided missile. She should have had a heroic end, perhaps sinking as she fired the final conquering salvoes of a great sea battle. Instead, her end was ignoble, but yet more memorable. The book tells about her breaking loose on her final voyage, foundering on Cornish rocks, the heroic saving of her crew, and then it tells of her salvage and dismantling – perhaps the most difficult and complex such task ever undertaken in British waters. The salvage was at once blunderful and brilliant, taking nine years of hard work and innovation albeit with some failures and setbacks, but finally successful.

The author is a leading authority on the history of dismantling and demolition of ships. He provides enough detail and meticulous research here to satisfy even the information-hungry nerds like me. But above all, this is a tale of naivety, ingenuity and courage. A good read indeed.

Ian Watson, *former Managing Director of Shipbreaking (Queenborough) – the last major UK shipbreaker, operating mainly at Cairnryan.*

HMS WARSPITE, *ready for war in April 1939.* *Topfoto*

INTRODUCTION

I have always been intrigued by the distinguished history of the battleship WARSPITE and more recently in the extraordinary tale of her final days. Wrecked off Cornwall on 23 April 1947 on her way to the breakers in Scotland, she was slowly broken up over the next nine years. What follows is the story of those years as this famous ship during this eventful and often difficult process, was re-floated in an amazing salvage operation and cut in two, before finally disappearing.

I undertook a Masters in UK Shipbreaking 1945/1995 at Newcastle University from 2018 to 2020. The Marine Technology Special Collection (MTSC) at the University possesses rich source material, including the records of many major UK shipbreakers as well as albums of relevant press cuttings. I enjoyed visiting the Local History Centre at Walsall to review the WARSPITE files of the Wolverhampton Metal Company (WMC) which had the major role in the salvage and demolition of this grand old ship in Cornwall. WMC had never broken up a ship before and has never done so since. Using this archive information, I had an article published on WARSPITE's sojourn in Cornwall.[1]

Then in anticipation of a talk on WARSPITE I was asked to do by the Cornwall Heritage Trust in February 2022, I realised, that despite extensive archive research, I had not been in contact with anyone involved with the ship in Cornwall. I thought of advertising in the local press for people with knowledge but realised that social media could be helpful, and it turned out to be a great success, with many contacts and photographs, often from people whose ancestors had worked on the wreck. My visit to Cornwall in February 2022 was also very helpful in terms of meeting people and making many new contacts, particularly at the talk, attended by a hundred or so. There was far more to report than I could possibly include in my lecture, so I decide to put pen to paper and write a history of WARSPITE's last nine years in Cornwall, endeavouring to pull all these sources together.[2]

This book includes a large number of photos, many of which are undated and their origins unclear. Black and white photos have generally been 'colourised' and I hope you will agree that this brings them to life rather well. Every effort has been made to ascertain copyright of photos. Unless stated otherwise, pictures are by the author. Any further information on WARSPITE in Cornwall would be of great interest.

Richard Holme
Saltwood, August 2023

---

[1] The sad end in Cornwall of WARSPITE – Warship World Vol 16 No 2. 2019.

[2] Some excellent books cover WARSPITE's service history. Two are Iain Ballantyne's 'WARSPITE from Jutland Hero to Cold War Warrior' (Pen and Sword, 2001) and 'Battleship WARSPITE' by V.E. Tarrant (Arms and Armour Press 1990). See also appendix 9.

CONTENTS

ABBREVIATIONS

MI	Metal Industries
MTSC	Marine Technology Special Collection, Newcastle University
Penlee	Penlee House Gallery and Museum, Penzance
Walsall	Local History Centre, Walsall
WMC	Wolverhampton Metal Company
WSPL	World Ship Photo Library

CHAPTER 1

DESTINED FOR BREAK UP?

WARSPITE had a most distinguished career in both world wars and was the most decorated ever Royal Navy ship. This valiant record continued into the latter stages of her operational life. On 6 June 1944, she was the first ship to open fire on D-Day, but then just a week later she was badly damaged by a mine off Harwich. Patched up further at Rosyth dockyard to continue bombardment duties she was already in a poor state from earlier war damage. Just one example was a German glider bomb off Salerno in September 1943, this had torn a hole in her bottom. This had been patched up with concrete in Gibraltar in December 1943.

It was no surprise then that like many of the older battleships, WARSPITE was placed in reserve before hostilities ceased during World War 2[3]. She was worn out from her war service – for example, one of her four 15-inch turrets was out of action, and one other could only fire intermittently. For this reason, in 1946, she was the first of the Royal Navy's fleet of operational battleships to be put up for disposal – the first of ten over the next two years as the old battle fleet was reduced in size.

In Number 3 Basin, Portsmouth dockyard in 1945. *Author's collection*

WARSPITE was moored at Spithead from 11 December 1944 to 25 June 1945 and then came into Portsmouth dockyard until 27 July 1945. It is likely that it was then that her 15-inch guns were removed by the 250-ton crane in Number 3 basin (see two images above) for possible re-use.[4] She then came again into Portsmouth

[3] She was reduced to Category B Reserve 12 March 1945 and to Category C in July 1945. (Tony Holtham).

[4] In fact, they were not re-used. An earlier 15-inch gun removed from WARSPITE in 1942 was though installed in the new battleship HMS VANGUARD.

dockyard from 9 January to 11 March 1947, presumably for final preparations for her tow to the breakers, Metal Industries (MI) and then out to Spithead again where she presented a sad sight:

She lies on her anchors on the Motherbank, a red ruin of rust and neglect, like an Indian queen painted grotesquely for her funeral pyre. Fussy little tugs chaffer around her like old clothes men bargaining for her shroud. But not a sound of protest from the old lady. You climb up the crazy makeshift ladder. You reach the top and your boot heel skids on a brass foot plate. Through the Verdigris, you read the name WARSPITE.[5]

MI was one of the UK's two largest shipbreakers and paid £101,275 for the ship and insured her for the trip to their yard at Faslane, Scotland for £150,000. They expected to profit from her acquisition by selling her steel, non-ferrous metals, and other materials; appendix 7 shows their estimated outturn. As a matter of detail, unusually they bought her direct from the Admiralty rather than being contracted to break the ship by the steel industry's British Iron & Steel Corporation (Salvage) Ltd (BISCO) as would be normal.

Languishing at Spithead, with two of her sister ships, **QUEEN ELIZABETH**, and **MALAYA** behind her, all awaiting a similar fate. Alongside **WARSPITE** is either **MOORFIELD** or **MOORHEN**, adjusting bridles for the tow to Faslane. *MTSC*

WARSPITE left Spithead bound for Faslane on 20 April 1947. Her steel was sorely needed to assist a recovering economy; this appetite for steel is a feature, a driving force, behind much of this story. For her final voyage, WARSPITE was towed by two

[5] Manchester Evening News 15 April 1947. The treadplate survives, see Chapter 7.

tugs operated by MI, BUSTLER and METINDA III[6]. WARSPITE was under the command of a Captain Baxter (ex-Merchant Navy) who takes up the story:[7]

I arrived at Portsmouth some days before the vessel was due to sail and inspected her and made our arrangements to sign on my crew when they should arrive.

Now at this point we agreed that there should be two tugs to tow the vessel, the BUSTLER which is of a considerable horsepower and a smaller horsepower METINDA tug. The captain of the BUSTLER agreed to be in charge of all the technical part of the operation, and the crew arrived, and we signed on and we went on board WARSPITE. The crew consisted of a bo'sun, six ABs, one cook, a donkey man and myself being nine hands in all.[8] It was purely what is known in the Navy as a C and M party, care and maintenance party only as the vessel had no power whatsoever. She had an anchor but once it was down it had to stay down; it couldn't be hauled up.

So off we duly sailed on the afternoon of April 20th in the early afternoon we went, and everything appeared to be going very well, the wind was roundabout southerly, not much wind, force three, about 15 miles an hour, slight to moderate sea, quite good steaming weather and nothing untoward at all; everything under control and off we went.[9]

It was noted that there had been no:

flourish or ceremony in this departure. The WARSPITE hoisted no colour flags, and no marine band played her out of harbour, as had been a custom on the hundreds of other departures she had made in her long and historic career. But to Captain Baxter this was just another of many similar tasks he had carried out.[10]

WARSPITE being cast off from her mooring buoy. *MTSC*

[6] BUSTLER was chartered by MI from the Admiralty, whereas MI had acquired METINDA III in 1946 for £40,000, ex EMPIRE JEAN, See appendix 8.
[7] BBC Radio Programme 1957 (Walsall)
[8] All other extant reports indicate eight, not ten, were on board WARSPITE on the final voyage.
[9] BBC Radio Programme 1957
[10] BBC Radio Programme 1957

The tugs **ST MELLONS** and **EMPIRE CHARLES** taking **WARSPITE**, out to Spithead probably in March 1947, from Portsmouth dockyard. Note her 15-inch guns have been removed.

Author's collection

Sadly, the great ship and her two attendant tugs were hit by increasingly heavy weather as they passed the Lizard Point in Cornwall.

The tow was lost and WARSPITE drifted on to rocks at Cudden Point, Mount's Bay. At high tide on 23 April, she drifted closer in and was stuck on the rocks at Prussia Cove with a list to port and her bows well down. The Penlee lifeboat, W & S, came out and braved the 30 foot plus waves and confined conditions, to rescue the crew in a rescue adjudged the most heroic of 1947 throughout the UK. A full account of the wreck and the amazing lifeboat rescue can be found in Appendix 3.

The lead tug **BUSTLER** in 1946 *WSPL*

The smaller tug towing WARSPITE, **METINDA III**, seen after rebuilding. *United Towing Society*

Quite a storm; **WARSPITE** seen (just!) from one of the towing tugs. *MTSC*

The Penlee lifeboat **W & S** rescuing the WARSPITE crew. *painting by Geoffrey Huband RSMA*

The RNLI awarded Coxswain Edwin 'Eddie' Madron, their Silver Medal for gallantry, while Motor Mechanic Johnny Drew, received the Bronze Medal. The rest of the heroic crew were awarded the thanks of the RNLI on vellum – Second Coxswain Joseph Madron, (brother of Coxswain Eddie Madron) Bowman John 'Jack' Worth, Assistant Motor Mechanic Jack Wallis and lifeboatmen Abe Madron (another brother of Coxswain Eddie Madron), Benjamin Jeffery and Clarry Williams.

Coxswain Eddie Madron and Motor mechanic Johnny Drew. *Edwina Reynolds Collection*

It was a dreadful storm, and on the same wild night the entire crew of eight of the Mumbles lifeboat EDWARD, PRINCE OF WALES were tragically lost as were the crew of 39 of the liberty cargo ship SAMTAMPA, the ship she was endeavouring to assist.

The wreck of this great ship was unfortunate; Britain badly needed her 25,000 tons[11] or so of scrap. There seems to be no basis for blaming Captain Baxter or the tugs, in those days advance forecasting of weather was not as refined today.

[11] Appendix 7 shows that MI estimated net recoverable scrap would be 24,700 tons. Press reports frequently refer to a higher tonnage, quite possibly confused by reference to the ship's full load displacement in service.

Perhaps MI should have arranged for three tugs to undertake the tow, rather than two. Anecdotal evidence suggests this was sometimes the case for battleships.

In the meantime, the wreck of WARSPITE was exposed to the elements.

For months, WARSPITE lay in Prussia Cove, being battered, and pounded by every storm. Her hull groaned as she worked on the rocks. Rivets were forced out of her with explosions like gun shots. There had been some fears that if the ship broke up, any fuel oil in her tanks might leak out and ruin the local lobster and crab fishing and foul beaches but this never happened. Instead, the stranded ship brought considerable profit to the neighbourhood. Sightseers, by the hundred, invaded the Cove and with the coming of the holiday season these became thousands. Farmers did well in parking fees, stalls were set up to market souvenirs and the fishermen did excellent business, running boat trips around the ship. Many old Navy men came to look down on the wreck of the ship they had known as the pride of the Royal Navy.[12]

The tug **BUSTLER** fires a line by rocket towards **WARSPITE**, probably 22 April 1947. *MTSC*

[12] BBC Radio Programme 1957.

The lifeboat **W & S** approaches **WARSPITE** 23 April 1947. *Penlee*

At Prussia Cove, probably April 1947. Note rear 'Y' 15-inch turret and teak deck. *MTSC*

A joint report by Captain Shotton of Lloyd's and Commodore Tom Mackenzie of MI quickly confirmed by 30 April 1947 that the old ship was a constructive total loss. The insurers paid up the insured amount of £150,000 to MI and looked to sell the wreck.

Contemporary press comment confirmed the insurers' view that it was impossible to salvage the ship. For example, an authoritative shipping periodical concluded that:

It seems improbable that the WARSPITE will ever be refloated. To salve her from such a situation would be so formidable and expensive an operation that her value as scrap would never cover the cost. Possibly her present owners might do a certain amount of dismantling where she lies during the summer months, but even that may not prove to be an economic process. So, the WARSPITE seems likely to be left where she now lies, a national monument until those inexorable shipbreakers, rock and storm have eventually done their work.[13]

Appendix 4 lists some excellent evocative contemporary newsreels exist of the great ship stranded at Prussia Cove and these can be found on YouTube.

The busy shipbreaking yard at Hayle, Cornwall in 1921, yet not big or deep enough to take WARSPITE. *MTSC*

At the time, the UK shipbreaking industry was the biggest in the world, partly as it had a monopoly in acquiring Royal Navy ships (and UK registered merchant vessels) for demolition. However, at the time, besides Faslane, only Inverkeithing on the Firth of Forth and Dalmuir on the Clyde could accommodate a ship as big as WARSPITE. All these yards were very shortly to begin breaking up other battleships

[13] Shipbuilding and Shipping Record 1947 p427.

so had little appetite to go to the trouble of somehow salvaging WARSPITE, and towing her to one of their yards, hundreds of miles away. Although MI's rival TW Ward had a shipbreaking yard at nearby Hayle in Cornwall, this was not nearly big enough to take WARSPITE. Admittedly in the late 1920s and early 1930s, MI had salvaged much of the German fleet scuttled at Scapa Flow in 1919 and taken the salvaged ships to their base at Rosyth for break up in what ultimately turned out to be a very profitable project. However, these ships had been scuttled in relatively sheltered waters, not wrecked in open sea, and were thus much easier to salvage. Moreover, shipbreakers before 1939 had been much less busy so had ample capacity to take on these ships.

CHAPTER 2

PRUSSIA COVE 1947

A Daily Express reporter was taken on board the wreck by fishermen with local knowledge:

Running out in the swell after the gale abated in their little boat the SECRET, we were the first to scramble aboard the WARSPITE. Her hawsepipes were awash and she has heeled well over to port. These men know every rock below the surface, and they showed me with soundings how she is resting on the great knob of rock about two thirds of the way along her hull with her bow in deeper water and nothing supporting her to seaward. With a paraffin lamp, I clambered through her lower decks, boiler rooms, turbine rooms, gear rooms, my way often barred by flooded compartments. She is holed many times and water was even spurting through the sides at surface level. They're not putting a watchman on board her in case she goes right over, and I wouldn't advise trippers to loiter on board. My opinion is that at a conference in London tomorrow she will be accepted as a total loss, and it will be later seen whether some concern will pay Lloyd's to salvage what is possible of her non-ferrous metals. [14]

Fishing boats at Boat Cove near the stricken ship. *Author's collection*

The unsupported bow, mentioned by the reporter, was to give rise to problems later for the shipbreakers. In the meantime, thousands of tourists flocked to see the wreck of WARSPITE, easily visible from the cliffs.

Animated scenes were witnessed at Prussia Cove on Sunday when immense crowds came from all parts to see the wrecked battleship. Cars poured into the little cove and although several fields were opened as car parks they were filled to capacity and the lane leading from the main road was jammed with vehicles of all kinds. A special detachment of police was on the spot all day to deal with traffic and endeavour to keep the line free.[15]

[14] Daily Express 28 April 1947.

[15] Western Morning News 29 April 1949.

A good view of the ship from clifftop. *MTSC*

Many family holiday snaps were taken on the clifftop with the wreck in the background, see one example above. Indeed, on the author's most recent trip to Prussia Cove in February 2022, he met a lady who had been photographed at this very spot as a nine-year-old, way back in 1947.

The Tunstall-Behrens family (see appendix 6.4) owned the land at Prussia Cove (and indeed still do). It is known as the Porth-en-Alls estate. The Tunstalls were far from happy at the large number of visitors but generously built a public car park for them which survives to this day.

On 19 August 1947, the insurers accepted an offer of £25,000 for the wreck from Bristol scrap merchant R.H. Bennett, acting in conjunction with another Bristol scrap trader A.J. Brewis. Bennett's business was long established, founded in fact in 1868. However, neither had any experience of shipbreaking, so to start on a battleship was somewhat ambitious, to say the least. They did not board WARSPITE prior to making their bid. (MI, having received their insurance monies, had unsuccessfully bid £7500 to the insurers for the wreck and had envisaged using a local contractor to extract non-ferrous and other valuable arisings.)

View from the shore, note the bows are well down and Sea View Cottage where workers were later accommodated. *Penlee*

The storm is only just abating on 25 April 1947, two days after **WARSPITE** went on the rocks. *Topfoto*

A bystander viewing the great ship as the storm abates. *Topfoto*

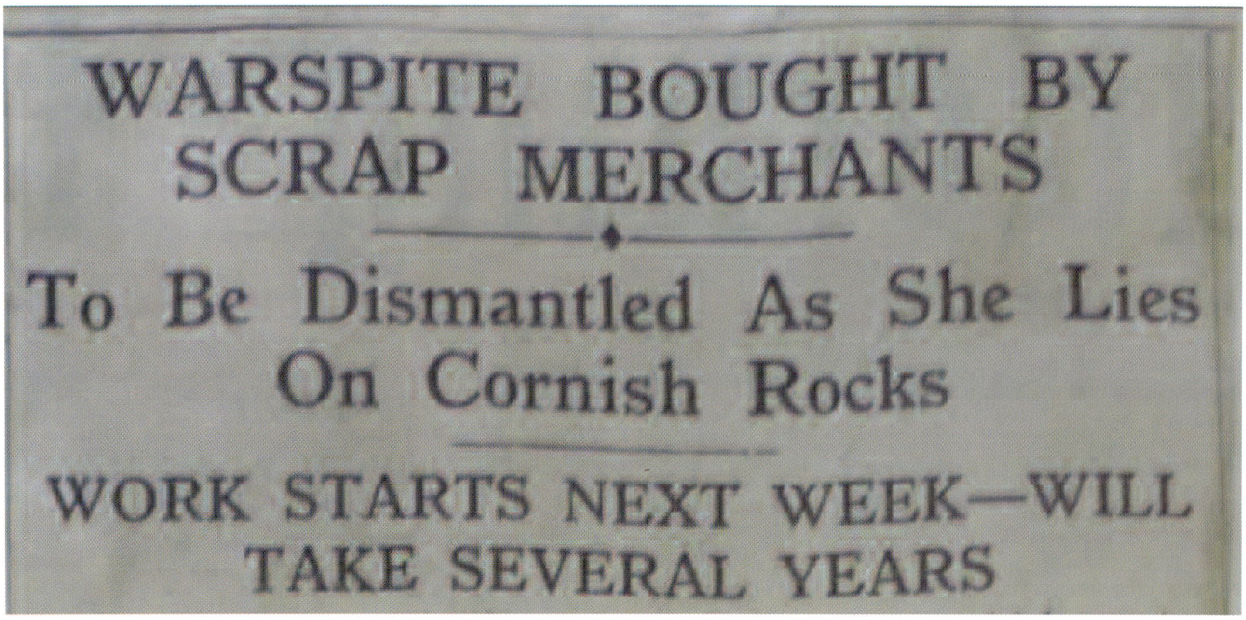

WARSPITE BOUGHT BY SCRAP MERCHANTS

To Be Dismantled As She Lies On Cornish Rocks

WORK STARTS NEXT WEEK—WILL TAKE SEVERAL YEARS

It was clear they were also a small operation as Mr. Bennett confessed:

We are a small company - myself, my two sons and Mr. Brewis. The bulk of the metal we get will go to the Midlands and South Wales. We also hope to be able to sell some of the machinery. The dismantling operations will begin on Monday. The work, which is likely to be difficult and hazardous in winter, is expected to last two or three years. Mr. Bennett said: I don't want to say how much we paid for her. That's a trade secret. . .? Denying that it was intended to run a temporary railway from the coast near the WARSPITE. *Mr. Bennett said their scheme was to work first from lighters and then shift the hulk to a shipyard.*[16]

TELEPHONE 77434 (2 LINES)

RHB

R·H·BENNETT

TELEGRAMS SCRAP BRISTOL

IRON, METAL & MACHINERY MERCHANT

LOWER KEYFORD WORKS
FROME
TELEPHONE FROME 2276

MINISTRY OF SUPPLY
NON-FERROUS METAL
LICENCE No. 1120/51

60 & 61 · FEEDER ROAD
BRISTOL
Established 1868

144 WEST STREET
BEDMINSTER BRISTOL
TELEPHONE BRISTOL 63106

Little is known about Bennett and Brewis, although some extant correspondence reveals their addresses and colourful letterheads. Bennett also had a car trading business.

The acquisition by the Bristol scrap merchants at first sight seems bizarre but becomes understandable when it is understood they were backed by a listed company, the Wolverhampton Metal Company (WMC). Indeed, WMC agreed to lend Bennett and Brewis £15,000 of the £25,000 purchase price. This was expressed as an advance payment for non-ferrous metals (e.g., copper) from the wreck: they had agreed to sell all such metals arising to WMC at an advantageously low price of £40/ton. Open market price was at least a third more than this. Bennett and Brewis had previously been suppliers to WMC. Extensive press reports of the Bristol acquisition curiously make no mention of WMC's involvement.

TELEPHONES
BRISTOL 26805
(After business Hours) 67901

CONTRACTOR TO H.M. GOVERNMENT

MEMBER
NFSM
NATIONAL FEDERATION OF SCRAP IRON & STEEL MERCHANTS

TELEGRAMS
"RESCRAP, BRISTOL"

SCRAP STEEL
IRON & METAL
MERCHANT

A.J. BREWIS,
2 CLARE STREET,
BRISTOL, I

PLANT AND
MACHINERY
DISMANTLED

AJB/M/W 1206

20th December, 1951.

---

[16] Western Morning News 29 July 1948.

In calmer waters but well down by the bows and listing to port, a photo probably from April 1947.
Author's collection

WMC was a major reprocessor of non-ferrous metals and had recently floated on the London Stock Exchange. Founded in the 1890s, it was managed by the James family. T.C. James, grandson of the founder, was managing director. By 1974, WMC was noted as the UK's leading producer of non-ferrous ingots. Although steel formed the greater part of the weight of any naval ship like WARSPITE and could be readily recycled, it was the non-ferrous metals that were the most valuable. As Appendix 7 shows, steel in 1946 could fetch £3.40/ton whereas copper would realise £53. WMC director Joe Barnes was involved in estimating the non-ferrous outturn from WARSPITE.

One unusual aspect after the wrecking was that the four huge 15-inch gun turrets were all trained to starboard, whereas they were all pointing bow and stern on leaving Portsmouth. Presumably this arose from the ship lurching sharply to port when she hit the rocks at Prussia Cove. It was certainly not due to later work by the breakers, as the turrets had moved into this position as soon as she was wrecked. Indeed, the turrets were moving somewhat during the storm as evidenced by images on pages 19 to 25 taken at different times in April 1947.

T.C. James, WMC managing director (left), and (right) other directors of WMC. *Walsall, J. Wilce*

Aerial view in May 1947, houses in background on the Porth-en-Alls estate include two used later to house workers on the ship *Topfoto*

Stern of **WARSPITE** on 23 August 1947 before demolition work started. *M. Crowdy/ WSPL*

C. Penrose

The Bristol scrap merchants appointed a local man, Ted Penrose (*pictured left*), to head day to day operations which began on 2 September 1947. A former officer on WARSPITE, Reg Coote, met Penrose as he toured his old ship in October 1947:

Captain of HMS WARSPITE on her last voyage will be Ted Penrose, short, dark, "born and bred in boats", native of Hayle in St Ives Bay. Ted is head of an advance party of 35 Cornish workmen aboard WARSPITE, fast on the rocks at Prussia Cove, Cornwall, stripping the Old Lady of the Navy for her final trip. She is to be towed to a more sheltered spot to be broken up without the risk of losing a single bolt. Under his command Ted Penrose will have a "break up" crew of 200 men. "Many old sea captains would be glad, I know, to see the Old Lady go to an honourable and dignified end in deep water, but not me," said Penrose. And judging by the determined way in which he and his party have set about their task, operation "break up" will not fail. Rough weather will not prevent them pressing ahead with the work during the winter. Next week a Blondin rope with breeches buoy is to be slung between the listing ship and the rugged shore so that the workmen can be brought off in the gales; and walkie-talkie apparatus is to be installed to speed up communication. Only connection with the mainland at the moment is by the small boat which took me out today to the 32,000-ton wreck. For me it was a moving experience. I had made just such a trip as this many times before when I lived in the famous "Battle Wagon" in the heyday of her glory. The nostalgic moment brought memories and images tumbling into my mind; Gib, Alex, Malta, Sicily, Salerno, the surrender of the "Eyetye" fleet; men I had known intimately, men whose names I could not now remember – laughing, talking, drinking. Ghosts of a thousand sailors. I picked my way aft over the littered and rusted deck towards the captain's cabin that "holy of holies" where a line of famous officers from Jutland to D-Day had hatched their plans. At the cloth-less table I found Mr Penrose, eating Irish stew. "My job", Mr Penrose explained to me as he showed me round my old ship, "is to make her a total recovery; to save every bit of her for scrap. I was in Admiralty Salvage during the war, but this is the biggest job I have ever handled!" We went down to my old cabin, now a stripped, gloomy cell, with a panel missing from the door, and a pool of black oil on the deck. It was in another world, it seemed – another life – when I used to be sweating on that bunk, wondering, and dreaming – dreaming the same dreams that thousands of sailors have dreamed between those decks. What thoughts and prayers the Old Lady must have listened to? "The wood will be sold and the metal smelted down," Mr Penrose was saying, "the whole job of breaking her up will take a good five years..." I could almost hear Nelson heave a sigh from the top of his column."[17]

Workers clamber on 15-inch A turret 2 September 1947. This must have been for the cameras, as the turret was not to be demolished until the following year. *Topfoto*

Note that Penrose, involved in Admiralty salvage during World War 2, was suggesting that WARSPITE could be refloated and taken away to a more suitable location for breaking up. His background was in salvage not shipbreaking, so he must have found the WARSPITE project particularly challenging. The author was saddened to hear from his family that he died soon after involvement with WARSPITE, possibly in part due to stress invoked from managing this difficult operation. He is not mentioned after January 1948, but his involvement may well have continued after this.

For the workforce, a six-day week was normal, while average wages were £8 per week. WARSPITE's own remaining 10-ton electric seaplane crane was activated,

[17] Reynolds News 28 April 1947.

proving useful in shifting scrap, but was fixed and with a limited capacity. There were around 32 workers initially, rising to 60 in 1948. Some of them lived in Sea View House and the Haven nearby, properties on the Porth-En-Alls estate, at Prussia Cove, see Appendix 6.4. The work was hard, but morale seems to have been good as noted a little later by one worker:

Union hours mean nothing to us ...we know that the job has to be done and we are working like mad to do it. The company pays us and feeds us well and we are all very happy.

Ten months had gone by from the start of demolition, when a press report in July 1948 highlighted the seemingly excellent progress made to date:

With her superstructure almost gone, HMS WARSPITE at Prussia Cove is losing all semblance of a battleship. Her breakers, Messrs R.J. Bennett, and Sons (Bristol) are meeting with success in dismembering the massive steel frame. Great strides have been made in tearing the ship to pieces in recent weeks and the scrap men are still doggedly working their way down into the dank bowels of the vessel. Thousands of tons of seawater and black oil still hold possession of much of her, especially for'ard where her nose lies plunged down. Performing what must be one of the filthiest tasks in the world, the men are accepting their daily lagging of black ooze as something inevitable in taking the pumps deeper and deeper below tide level. Definite hopes are now entertained that during the next three years the whole of WARSPITE's 30,000 tons of metal will be recovered piecemeal for the benefit of the nation. In a tour of the salvage operations, on Monday, a West Briton reporter was given an idea of the engineering skill, brawn, and grit necessary to save the fortune in metal from the sea's clutches. The ship is indeed worth a fortune in terms of scrap, Mr R.H. Bennett, senior partner of the firm said "If we can get it all away as scrap, she will be worth about £250,000" ... Over 60 men are employed, the weekly payroll is in the region of £500 and since Messrs Bennetts became the owners last August, costs have run up to £17,000. "the more suitable men we find to do the work, the more we shall put on." To date the operations have yielded 2000 tons of mixed metals. Weather and equipment delays have been many but there is now a regular tug ferry service to Penzance harbour, where a crane hoists the mammoth chunks of steel onto the quayside. This scrap is then loaded onto lorries and taken to the railway station about 100 yards away for reloading on to trucks for South Wales and the Midlands. Recent negotiations with Penzance Town Council to extend a railway track already existing along the quay so that the rail trucks can be shunted right up to the salvage tenders were unsuccessful. Mr Bennett said the present system of having to reload twice within a distance of 100 yards or so was greatly delaying the despatch of the metal as well as adding considerably to labour costs. "The Ministry of Supply is continually asking us to get on with the production of the scrap" he said "and I am convinced that with the extension of this piece of railway line from the quayside to the station the loading could be vastly speeded up."

Workers on the forecastle 2 September 1947. Note the massive bridge structure to rear, installed as part of the 1934-37 reconstruction at Portsmouth. *Topfoto*

Bow view; what appears to be a gaping hole on the port side is in fact a recess for the 6-inch gun casemates. *Author's collection*

Operations are now controlled from a permanent headquarters ashore – a house in which the walls are lined with blueprints of WARSPITE's interior. These plans are studied regularly for many compartments are still dangerously flooded. At high tide her nose just clears tide level. WARSPITE's wealth of metals include nickel and stainless steel, copper, brass, gun metal, lead and aluminium in large quantities. The most valuable metals are worth about £80 a ton of scrap at the quayside although the average price of a ton of the ship as a whole is estimated at £7. The cutting up of her

four huge gun turrets estimated at 1350 tons each is itself a notable salvage feat. Directing operations at Prussia Cove is Mr Robert Bennett who is most optimistic about the future. "Everybody seem to be doubtful whether she would stand the winter here," he said, "but there was never any doubt as far as I was concerned. Since last winter a crack has appeared right across the ship in front of the bridge but Mr Bennett explained that this meant she was now completely bedded on the rocks which is also good. When the superstructure had finally disappeared work would continue down inside. An attempt might be made when nothing, but her shell remained to patch up her scarred holes, but it will be at least two years before this decision would be called for. Many of the present 48 fitters, burners and labourers working on board the ship come from as far away as Redruth, Camborne, and Falmouth each day. Including overtime, the working week often extends beyond 60 hours. The firm's lorries bring them to Prussia Cove and return them to their homes. A canteen has been provided locally. [18]

Working conditions on WARSPITE at this time were not easy. Many of the workers would have to wade through oil in the course of their duties and after their Porth-en-Alls living quarters were vacated, it took the owners several weeks to clean up the oil left behind in the houses (see appendix 6.4). Warships, like WARSPITE, at this time would have incorporated harmful asbestos, capable of causing serious health issues, longer term. No contemporary reports of this relating to the ship were found, but some families did later fear early deaths were due to asbestos. There was undoubtedly fuel oil on board, although most should have been removed when in Portsmouth dockyard. Oil was a worry throughout the period of demolition but thcrc is no evidence of major oil pollution.

In January 1948, the Duke of Kent visited *(left)* and is possibly seen on the open bridge, at bottom right. He was rather young at the time and was in the area, receiving tuition from Giles St Aubyn at St Michael's Mount. The image gives a good view of the features on the open bridge. Images on page 57 also depict the young Duke's visit.

Walsall

[18] West Briton 8 July 1948 (extracts).

In November 1947, Bennett had transferred the WARSPITE hulk and associated operation to a limited company, Western Salvaging Company Ltd (WSL), presumably to get the protection of limited liability for this risky operation. WSL was owned by himself and a George Bennett, assumed to be his son. As noted above, a Blondin wire (breeches buoy) was established between the cliffs and the ship in October 1947. Workers would travel out to the ship to start their day's work using this, when the weather was too rough for boats to be used. It was designed by engineer Duncan Nicholson (appendix 6.5 for his background) who was to work on the WARSPITE project until 1953. It looks hazardous even on a quiet day.

Three locals, Doreen and Mary Reynolds and their cousin Audrey Littlecott. *Sarah Field*

A visit to the Blondin wire was a memorable experience, as one reporter recounted:

AERIAL RAILWAY TO WARSPITE, Plank as Seat. DIZZY JOURNEY OVER SEA. A trip to the old battleship WARSPITE, wrecked in Prussia Cove; has taken on a new thrill these days for continuous rough weather of the last few weeks has made it impracticable to reach the ship by boat, and the shipbreakers have rigged an aerial railway between the ship and the top of the cliff and make the journey by pulley and a plank. I had a trip on it yesterday... not because I wanted to go to the WARSPITE that way, but because our photographer Tom Roskrow wanted to get a picture of somebody actually doing this high-wire act. When we arrived nobody else was travelling on the wire because it was between shifts, and as Roskrow would not go away without his picture I was offered for sacrifice. Believe me, of all the positions in which it is possible to be photographed, dangling from a pulley over a cliff is not the most enjoyable. LIKE A GULL. The railway comprises a heavy wire hawser which stretches in a long curve between the ship and the shore. At the shore end it is clamped to a stout post which is driven into the cliff top and anchored by a ship's anchor embedded in concrete. The "carriage" which runs along this, is an ordinary pulley with a wire strap to which is attached to a 3ft plank for a seat. You sit on this, a man loops a rope around your waist, the crew pull on the hauling line and away you go over the edge of the cliff and swoop-like a gull over the sea. Soon this method of transport is to be improved... One of these is a huge basket in which passengers of the future will be transported along the line. But this is a heavy contrivance and requires to be power-driven. The motor for it has arrived but has not yet been set up... Alongside the shore end of the wire, the shipbreakers have built an ingenious hut out of the WARSPITE's deck plating, and in spite of its rough and ready construction it is surprisingly warm inside even without a fire. A ship's telephone has been installed which gives communication with the warship. There are now 32 men engaged in breaking WARSPITE but in spite of their labour there is very little outward change in the battleship's appearance. During recent gales she has been severely battered by huge seas and a crack has developed in her starboard side. Officials of the shipbreakers' company, however, told me that they do not regard this as serious. It is certainly not dangerous.[19]

Despite this optimism, this crack was later to prove troublesome to the shipbreakers. The post used to anchor the shore side of the Blondin wire survives and is pictured and discussed in Chapter 7.

Two views of the Blondin wire in operation. *Authors collection, Topfoto*

During a fierce storm in January 1948, a Second World War mine passed within a hundred yards of WARSPITE, what an irony if German efforts had damaged her yet again. The awful winter weather did not stop work on the ship, but scrap could not always be easily removed for resale. Once eight of the workforce stayed on board for two nights to get important work done apparently, not because 70 mph winds were making the Blondin wire hazardous. The Blondin in due course became mechanised and a basket holding four was introduced.[20]

[19] Western Morning News 1947
[20] Evening Standard 21 January 1948.

A stern view, maybe late 1948. X turret is being cut down and two derricks set up, one maybe a former ammunition derrick. *Negus Penzance*

WSL generated £10,000 of income by stripping the upper works of the ship and selling 2,000 tons or so of metal. The image above is a rare image of the ship at a time WSL were actively breaking up the ship. The funnel and bridge had soon disappeared; the steel was relatively thin but the turrets were a tough nut to crack. WSL were getting into financial trouble. Costs of £17,000 were higher than income of £10,000. Moreover, WMC feared that non-ferrous metals were being sold direct to third parties rather than to themselves at the agreed discounted price. By summer 1948, the workforce had expanded to at least 60 (working often a 60-hour week) with a weekly payroll cost of £500. With the encouragement of the Ministry of Supply, the railway at Albert Pier was lengthened to allow easier landing and travel on of scrap. There is an early hint at this early stage that the wreck might be refloated as her bulkheads were thought to be intact.[21] WSL looked to sell the WARSPITE wreck through an intermediary for up to £150,000, a fanciful price perhaps but even so there was some interest from the Belgian government.

The work was proving onerous as recounted later:

Working at Prussia Cove was extremely difficult. Everything had to be cut away in small pieces and got away from underfoot by Blondin cable to the cliff, and in small boats to the quay at Penzance. The usual method of dismantling a vessel of this size is to work on it at the breaker's yard, where cranes, cutting equipment, power and so on, are readily available, and the job can be done in something like a year. After

[21] West Briton 8 July 1948.

months of difficult work at Prussia Cove, the superstructure was removed, and they then came to the hardened steel of the gun turrets. Cutting away this nickel chrome steel slowed progress considerably, and the work became more and more expensive as time went on. Eventually, in May 1949, the Wolverhampton Metal Company took over complete control of the WARSPITE, *and we called in a firm of salvage experts to survey her with the intention of re-floating her and taking her to the ship breaker's yard. By this time, the back of the* WARSPITE *had been broken, and a split 2' wide had opened up on her deck.*[22]

The hulk, well cut down 25 February 1949. *M. Crowdy/ WSPL*

In early 1949, WSL had indeed been in serious financial trouble, with their debts including £12,000 to the bank, £7,000 to various creditors as well as £9,000 still to WMC. Liquidation of the company was on the cards. WMC were naturally concerned not only at recovery of their debt but also at the drying up of this substantial source of non-ferrous metal.

Discussions between WMC and WSL ultimately led to WMC acquiring the wreck in a complicated deal. The sale price is not wholly clear but was in the region of £30,000. This included WMC paying off WSL's creditors and bank debt. WMC promised to pay a further amount, under a gentleman's agreement, of as much as £25,000, to the Bristol scrap dealers if the venture turned out to be financially successful.

WMC estimator Joe Barnes (see appendix 6.5. for background) was involved in calculating what WMC should pay. WSL had acquired the wreck for £25,000 – although this figure was not disclosed publicly at the time and may not have been known to WMC.

[22] Frank Wilson of WMC in BBC 1957 Radio broadcast

The upperworks well cut down 25 February 1949 and an unobstructed view of the Blondin wire. The starboard hangar on the hulk was retained and useful for storage and shelter.

M. Crowdy/WSPL

In July 1949, WMC engaged the services of P. Bauer (Salvage) Ltd (a business headed by Philip Bauer), and they were to act as contractors until January 1952. Philip Bauer (pictured left – *I MacQuarrie collection*) started his business, selling salvaged cargo when he was just 20 years old. He then started ship salvage around the coast of Britain and abroad, particularly in France. There he worked on the D-Day beaches, where many ships had been abandoned. Bauer is also believed to have undertaken salvage work as far afield as Israel and South America. WMC obtained good references on Bauer and were aware that they had been engaged in several successful salvage operations, including one for the British Tanker Co Ltd on the Thames. Bauer employed the existing workforce and paid nearly all project costs. They were reimbursed for these expenses plus a small percentage (5%, a 'cost plus' basis), with a profit share element. The latter varied over the period of their involvement but was a third at most.

CHAPTER 3

REFLOATED AND THE MOVE TO MARAZION 1950

The Bauer salvage team had hoped to refloat WARSPITE as early as October 1949 although they feared she might break in two, once afloat. The wrecked ship needed to be patched up and water pumped out of all her compartments by compressors to provide necessary buoyancy. Images taken in February 1949 and up to July 1950 (and even beyond) show no obvious change in the hulk's appearance. This was because the workforce was entirely engaged in getting WARSPITE ready for re-floating. There was to be no dismantling for scrap until late 1950 and hence no revenue for WMC in this difficult period. A big investment therefore in salvage costs accruing to WMC as well as their purchase cost of the ship without any reward imminent in the form of scrap sales. Monthly wage costs peaked at £750 in November 1949. Patching up WARSPITE for prospective refloating was a massive task as manager Neil Macdonald recounted:

We had to cut away all the ventilating system and all the pipelines, and that had to be sealed by welding and wooden plaques. The hatches had to be forced down and kept in position by strong bars to take the pressure but inside the compartments most of the work was done in airlocks and men had to work under pressure.

An undated photo shows diver Jim Craig looking to seal the engine room which has been underwater for at least two years, hence its state here! *Walsall*

A reporter explained further:

Men worked in the tomb-like compartments deep inside the ship, often underwater in diving suits. They had to cut away and seal every pipe hole and ventilation shaft, working in every sort of position. Oil in some of the compartments soiled and burnt them and made even the simple business of standing on the canted deck impossible. In the smaller compartments the heat and fumes were the most difficult to deal with. Another young Scot, Neil MacQuarrie shared the direction of this difficult and dangerous job with Macdonald.

MacQuarrie added:

Well, I should say the main difficulties were working under pressure in air locks, and diving in the engine rooms and boiler rooms. Inevitably there were accidents.

Shipbreaking can indeed be a dangerous business and on 15 March 1950, a tragic accident led to the death of John Lennie MacQuarrie. He was working with two others in an air sealed compartment below sea level when they were overcome by fumes. It transpired at the Inquest that exhaust fumes from the compressors were blown into the air intakes for that compartment.

Describing their action as "deeds of selfless heroism", Penzance borough coroner Mr John R Arromanches praised the rescuers on HMS WARSPITE today when he completed the inquest on 27 year-old John Lennie MacQuarrie who died trapped in a gas filled compartment in the warship on March 15. The coroner returned a verdict of "accidental death", saying "One must admire the quite selfless heroism with which everybody in this ship went to the rescue of the people who had been overcome in this chamber. Everybody was prepared to risk their lives without hesitation. Having heard all the evidence it is clear to me that an accident occurred in that these men were overcome by carbon monoxide poison due to the use of a petrol driven compressor and as a result of that accident, the deceased died due to an air embolism associated with Caisson's disease." Mr F.D.M. Hocking, county pathologist, said he found only 3 to 4% of carbon monoxide in MacQuarrie's blood whereas it required from 50 to 70% to be fatal. He considered that the carbon monoxide MacQuarrie had originally absorbed had been swept out of his body as a result of the sudden release of pressure when he was rescued. The blood in his blood vessels had been churned to froth and the vessels had a spongy feeling as if blown out by air, characteristic of death due to Caisson's disease when pressure is suddenly released. His death was in fact due to the blocking of the circulation by air bubbles. The fact that the men who had been left in the chamber survived so long when rescuers were overcome so quickly was probably due to the fact that when they became unconscious, they lay and breathed very shallowly whereas the rescuers were exerting themselves and breathing deeply. [23]

For their bravery in the episode, four of the heroic salvage crew Neil Macdonald, Neil MacQuarrie, Thomas Convery and James Craig were awarded the George Medal and two others (Herbert Bullen and Peter Hynes) the British Empire Medal (Civil). The citations for their hugely deserved awards, giving more detail on their bravery in this tragic episode, are to be found in Appendix 5.

NINE GASSED UNDER SEA IN WARSPITE HULK

By Daily Mail Reporter

[23] Falmouth Evening Press 5 April 1950.

A casualty being landed on the cliff from **WARSPITE** on 15 March 1950. *Topfoto*

The starboard seaplane crane vital for unloading scrap. *K. Macdonald collection*

In June 1950, Counsel's opinion was taken from barrister John Megaw as to the legal position if the WARSPITE was beached at nearby Marazion. Bauer, the contractors, seemed to be keen on this option while WMC were more cautious as to the legal and practical consequences. Counsel thought a beaching would probably not in itself technically be a trespass but there would be a trespass and nuisance to the landowner when workers crossed the beach to get to the ship. He postulated the beach becoming a breaker's yard and felt it best in practice to get the consent of the Crown, Duchy of Cornwall, and beach owner to any action. Otherwise, an injunction might successfully be obtained, requiring abandonment of operations due to the nuisance and likely noise.

The hulk on 7 July 1950 after the first attempt at refloating. *I. MacQuarrie collection*

At last, in July 1950, after months of almost continuous effort, WARSPITE was ready for refloating. For three days and three nights the compressors pumped air into the sealed compartments at either end of the ship. Salvage manager, Neil Macdonald, remembered:

As the ends became buoyant, a gap in the midship section formerly about 2 to 3 feet wide had now closed up to its original. You couldn't even get a penknife in. Well at our first attempt, we had to give up owing to weather conditions. We had her afloat, in fact she moved about 15 feet further up on the rocks. Although we knew she was afloat we were rather disappointed we didn't manage to pull her off. The weather conditions were so bad that the tug couldn't get a hawser aboard, so we had to wait until the next spring tides. We had to exhaust all the air and of course we had a lot of work to do; we kept sealing the decks during that period then a fortnight later. Yes, we had very nice weather, beautiful morning; we had the three tugs standing by and as soon as they got their hawsers aboard, I think, within 20 minutes we were leaving Prussia Cove.[24]

The first attempt at refloating WARSPITE had been on 5 July 1950. Bauer's trawler tug BARNET was present, but any tow would have been taken by the Devonport-based, Admiralty rescue tug FREEBOOTER which was 'on hand' as well as another tug, name unknown. It is quite surprising perhaps, the Royal Navy made FREEBOOTER available but maybe as a favour (given the continuing national steel shortage) or perhaps she was in the area anyway.

Success came on 29 July, 1950, as three tugs from United Towing of Hull, ENGLISHMAN, MASTERMAN and BRAHMAN towed the refloated WARSPITE away from the rocks at Prussia Cove, for a not insubstantial fee of £1800. Her departure from Prussia Cove was though joyful.

WARSPITE under tow of the United Towing tugs on 29 July 1950. *Topfoto*

[24] BBC Radio programme 1957.

The men cheer as **WARSPITE** moves away. *Ken Babbage collection*

As WARSPITE moved slowly away, she was cheered by some 200 or 300 people. The men in the coastguard lookout hoisted the Union flag and fired a rocket of farewell. The men on WARSPITE lined the decks, cheering and throwing into the air any articles of clothing which came to hand. Such was the general excitement on board that the engineers forgot to cut the cable on the Blondin carrier and as WARSPITE moved away the cable snapped like a piece of string. Because of air pressure trouble caused by a leak in number 4 Boiler Room, WARSPITE was beached at Marazion. The engineers will patch and seam the boiler room. Because of the angle which she had been lying in Prussia Cove, they had been unable to complete the job thoroughly. This course and overall reduction in the air pressure gave WARSPITE a decided list to port as she was towed across the bay. I went to board the WARSPITE when she was halfway across the bay doing a steady 3 knots. As I walked round the oil covered decks my eardrums nearly shattered by the noise of the air compressors, little groups of men stood chatting and smiling their faces thick with grease and dirt after a final night's work to ensure that everything would be ready for the attempt. Short bespectacled Mr Bauer said "We set out to do a job and we have done it." Mr Neil Macdonald, a tall and burly Scot, could not praise highly enough the willing and unstinted efforts of the men under him who had for months worked "at full pressure and often in the foulest imaginable conditions".[25]

[25] Western Morning News August 1950.

WARSPITE under tow 29 July 1950. *Penlee*

The tow to Marazion is recorded in evocative contemporary newsreel films, see appendix 4.7 and 4.8. Press reports suggested that the tugs had intended to tow WARSPITE to a shipbreaking yard in South Wales. However, there is no available evidence to substantiate that a Welsh yard there had agreed to take her, and, in any case, they would have struggled to accommodate a ship of her size. The only possible yard was Cashmores at Newport, but with its steep riverbank it is thought most unlikely that a warship of WARSPITE's size could be cut up there, even if there was room. Further, just prior to the 1950 refloating, they had received two cruisers HMS AJAX (arrived 13 November 1949) and HMS NORFOLK (19 February 1950) for break up so there would have been little or no room for WARSPITE.

WARSPITE was towed three and a half miles from Prussia Cove (foreground) to St Michael's Mount, in background.

P.Tunstall-Behrens

Comparative stern views at Spithead during 1946 (left) and in a reduced cut down state on her way to Marazion. Most of turrets and superstructure gone except hangar by 29 July 1950.

MTSC, Penlee

Compressors used to refloat **WARSPITE.** *Author's collection*

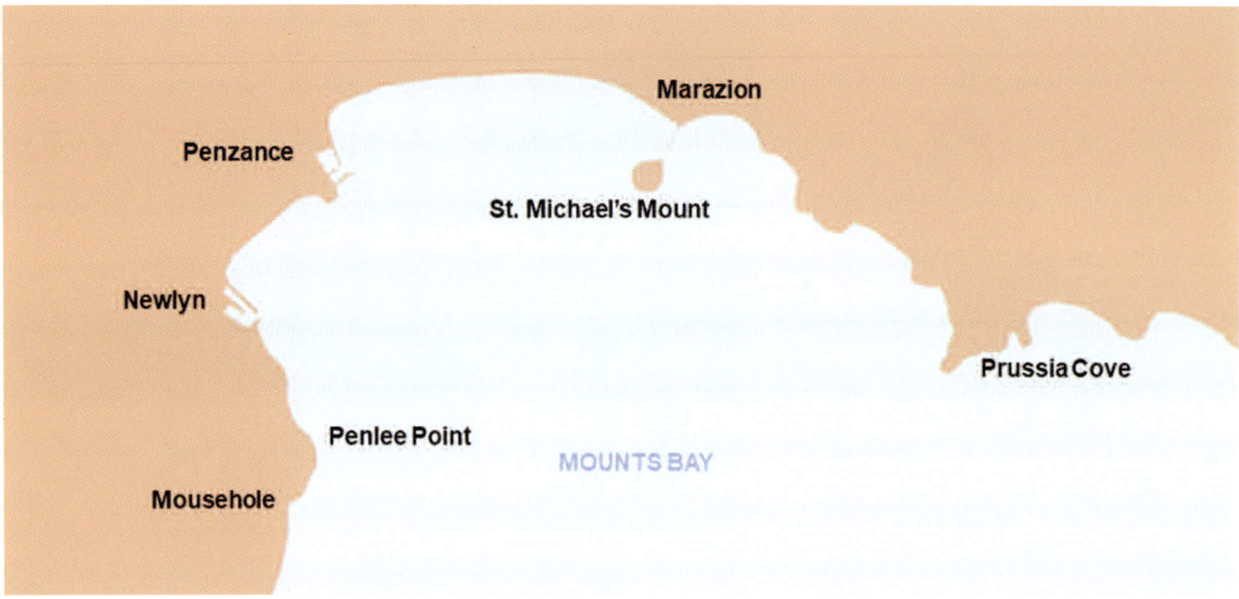

29 July 1950; WARSPITE is towed from Prussia Cove along to the west of St Michael's Mount. Penlee lifeboat station is just north of Mousehole. *K. Atkinson*

As noted above, WARSPITE was in fact towed only to Marazion due to an air leak in a boiler room, arriving to the west of St Michael's Mount before being towed further inshore later in the day. The taking of Counsel's opinion in June 1950 about beaching at Marazion suggests taking her there was always the plan, or a strong possibility. South Wales had been considered at an earlier stage as a destination, but insurance costs were prohibitive for a tow of 180 miles or so. The narrow confines of Cashmore's yard at Newport in South Wales were another issue as demonstrated by the image below of HMS SUFFOLK arriving there in June 1948.

MTSC

CHAPTER 4

TROUBLED TIMES AT MARAZION 1950-1953

As noted, the three Hull tugs took WARSPITE to Marazion and then attempted to move her closer inshore. WMC were keen to move WARSPITE away from Marazion to a more suitable site where the hulk could be cut up more easily on or nearer a beach in shallow sheltered water. They were disappointed that Bauer had not achieved this and this was to be a continuing frustration.

WARSPITE arrives by St Michael's Mount on 29 July 1950 with Newlyn in the background.
Penlee

ENGLISHMAN, one of three tugs used on 29 July, seen moored in Falmouth harbour.
United Towing Society

BRAHMAN leads the tow of the hulk past St Michaels Mount. *Penlee*

BRAHMAN, ex HM tug EMPIRE LARCH in the English Channel. *Tony Atkinson collection*

From the outset, Marazion authorities were also keen for the hulk to move on, as asserted by the Vice Chair of the Parish Council.

We shall be glad when the WARSPITE goes out of it altogether. Wherever she goes there is a certain amount of oil coming in on the beach, and you can see it now on the seaweed at Marazion.

Several ideas were put forward by WMC to move the hulk to another location where it could be beached to facilitate demolition and shelter from winter storms.

1. By Penlee quarry, Newlyn – lawyers for A.M.C protested at plans to beach by this, pointing out the adverse effects on Newlyn harbour from where A.M.C shipped out 300,000 tons of stone each year.
2. By the south pier at Newlyn – a letter of 23 September 1950 to the Newlyn Harbour Commissioners, following a meeting, proposed WARSPITE being beached there for a maximum of 12 months. Undertakings were given to protect Newlyn harbour particularly from silting. The hulk was to be lightened so as not to obscure fishing vessels' view of the Newlyn light. The letter mentions the Penlee quarry site being an alternative site but not as suitable as the seabed was quite possibly too soft.
3. There is reference to the hulk being moved to South Wales, either the Mumbles or Oxwich Bay.

Admiralty chart (extract from OCB 777) of Mount's Bay originally drafted 1891, updated to 1947. WARSPITE was wrecked at Prussia Cove to the east (right) side of the chart in April 1947 and moved to the west (centre) of St Michael's Mount in July 1950. There was much discussion about moving the hulk to Penzance and Newlyn further to the west. Then further south of Newlyn is Penlee lifeboat station. *UK Hydrographic Office*

The Ministry of Transport intervened in September 1950, protesting at the beaching proposals, and asserting that their permission would be needed before any such action was taken. They invoked section 34 of the Coast Protection Act 1949. Beaching was only to be permitted in an 'emergency measure' and a future beaching of WARSPITE was not likely at all to be such an occasion.

The Harbour Commissioners at Newlyn rejected out of hand, any proposals to use a site by their harbour. There were numerous difficulties, mainly concern as to impaired access for the fishing fleet into the harbour. Also, possible release of oil.

However, one Councillor reminded colleagues that steel from the hulk would provide munitions to help fight the war then under way in Korea (and which was to continue until July 1953).

Oil does not count. We have lost one boy in Korea already and if WARSPITE will make bullets to prevent that, oil does not matter.

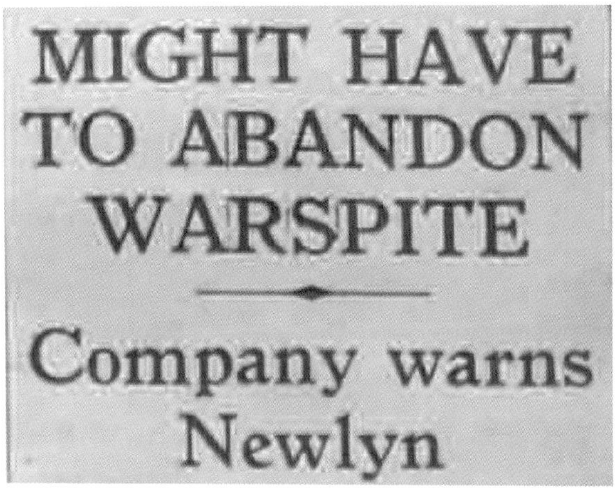
MIGHT HAVE TO ABANDON WARSPITE

Company warns Newlyn

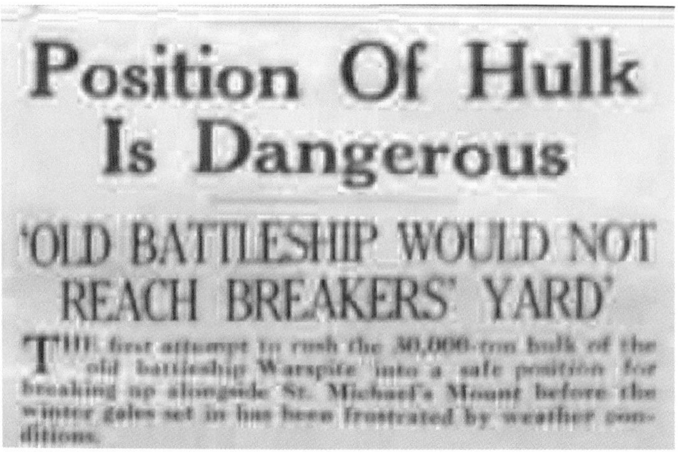
Position Of Hulk Is Dangerous

'OLD BATTLESHIP WOULD NOT REACH BREAKERS' YARD'

THE first attempt to rush the 30,000-ton hulk of the old battleship Warspite into a safe position for breaking up alongside St. Michael's Mount before the winter gales set in has been frustrated by weather conditions.

The authorities in Penzance were more amenable and discussed several sites including Roskilly beach, Penzance harbour and a site between the Gear Rock and Wherry Rocks on Penzance promenade. WMC conceded that the hulk was too big at present to be housed in the harbour itself and requested a site 2000 feet east of Penzance pier. A compromise was reached at 2500 feet east and Penzance awaited, no doubt, with a little trepidation, the relocation of WARSPITE there.

However, when the Hull tugs came again twice to move the hulk, it was to try to reach shallower water at Marazion, and, not surprisingly, the apparently more suitable site negotiated with Penzance. Three tugs TRADESMAN, SEAMAN and ENGLISHMAN came on 12 October 1950 and TRADESMAN again and MASTERMAN on 10 November 1950, for fees of £1250 and £700 respectively. Both occasions proved eventful as related below:

The first attempt to rush the 30,000 ton hulk of the old battleship WARSPITE into a safe position for breaking up alongside St Michael's Mount before the winter gales set in, has been frustrated by weather conditions. Daylight today found her lying in a dangerous position nearly broadside onto the sea. Bitterly disappointed, engineers who had worked through the night on board the ship to keep her in floating trim, stood on deck and gazed at the two tugs which were to do the work, riding at anchor 3 miles away, while time and tide ebbed away. Last night, time defeated a gallant fight to get WARSPITE into her new position. Despite pessimistic local opinions that WARSPITE had become so deeply embedded in the sand that she would not lift, the old hulk was as much afloat as any other ship. Responding to the pull of the tugs, she moved seawards. It was intended to take her into deep water, line her up for her new position, already marked by buoys close to St Michael's Mount and tow her back. The wind was strong, however and it was decided not to risk taking her clear of the shelter of the Mount. After she had moved forward about her own length the tugs tried to pull her towards the Mount, broadside on. Her stern swung about 200 feet but the bow could not be brought round against the wind, and the ebbing tide grounded her in a position, nearly broadside onto the sea. The salvage engineers were desperately keen to get her out of this dangerous position today but the weather was judged to be too stormy. Meantime their anxiety was increased by the fact that the air compressors on which the buoyancy of the great ship depends, had begun to give out after so many hours of continuous work. Two of them had stopped by this morning.... Fog screened the arrival of the tugs yesterday, until they were close up to WARSPITE and to the surprise of those onshore, they began to move her in the opposite direction from that planned by the Corporation. The decision to break her up in Mount's Bay means the abandonment of all thought of towing her to South Wales to be scrapped. This is another surprise. A member of the salvage firm told the Herald; "We really realise now she could not stand the strain of such a long trip. Having decided to break her up here we have to get her where we could put workmen aboard, and that at all states of tide and in all weathers. Newlyn having refused us; St Michael's Mount was the only possible alternative". Negotiations are going on with Lord St Leven's representative for permission to put a Blondin cable from the Mount to the WARSPITE, so that men and supplies can be conveyed to her by overhead wire as at Prussia Cove. Close alongside the harbour wall at St Michael's Mount, the first stage of demolition will be undertaken, later when she's been stripped to the water line, the WARSPITE may be towed close enough to the beach to enable workmen to approach her from the shore.[26]

The United Towing tug **MASTERMAN** on another assignment in 1951. *United Towing Society*

[26] Cornish Evening Herald 13 October 1950.

Moving her the next day unfortunately presented problems also.

For the second day in succession, a broken tow rope robbed a salvage crew of the success they deserved and the 30,000 tons ex-warship WARSPITE is still not in her final position in Mount's Bay for breaking up. It was nearly 2 hours of hard struggle last night before the old warship grounded again and the victory within reach became victory deferred. The struggle will be resumed this morning and it is confidently expected that the ship will then ground between the two buoys which have been set to mark her final resting place off the pier at St Michael's Mount. Three powerful tugs made last night's attempt. The air compressors which have been working for over 70 hours without stopping, gave the required buoyancy at about 6:30 pm and then began the first phase which was to bring the stern towards the open sea. Gradually the broadside to the fore position changed and towed by TRADESMAN and ENGLISHMAN the stern swung through a quarter circle. There followed the pull out to sea and gradually the giant moved, SEAMAN at the bows keeping her straight. ENGLISHMAN then pulled on the starboard quarter and with the other two gradually changing direction. WARSPITE was soon close to the Mount and in good position for the final phase. Then came disaster, the tow rope of ENGLISHMAN parted, and for 40 minutes this powerful tug was unable to take an active part. The salvage company's own ship, BARNET made an effort to save the position. Despite the heavy swell which crashed her against WARSPITE again and again, BARNET closed with the warship, put a rope aboard and endeavoured to push the vessel. But gradually WARSPITE drew away from the Mount so she was halfway back to her original position. Darkness fell before ENGLISHMAN managed to get a rope aboard WARSPITE again and joining TRADESMAN at the stern they pulled the ship toward land. The Mount slid by almost imperceptibly but the tugs could not stop the sideways pull on the huge hull and at 8:20 she again grounded.[27]

TRADESMAN pictured on the Humber in early 1960s. *United Towing Society*

[27] Western Morning News 15 October 1950

The unfortunate BARNET ended up being beached in the process and her remains can still be seen on the beach at Long Rock near Penzance, although there is some doubt as to the identity of the wreck.

Then further issues arose in attempts to move WARSPITE in November:
WARSPITE claimed another victim last night when the tug MASTERMAN went ashore on the Hogus rocks just as she was casting off from the hulk after two hours struggle with the TRADESMAN to get the 38,000-ton mass of steel nearer to St Michael's Mount. Fortunately, the sea was calm. The TRADESMAN tried for some time to pull the MASTERMAN off, but without success and subsequently left and anchored off Penzance. The MASTERMAN is apparently in no danger and her crew remain on board. She went ashore on a falling tide and will probably be refloated on next high water. No great advance was made in getting WARSPITE to her selected berth. The old warship was fully afloat once more and responded readily to the pull of the tugs. She was thought to have been brought in some 600 feet nearer the shore, but she appeared finally to have met some obstructions amidships and though she would pivot she made little lateral progress. WARSPITE still showing the effects of the recent flooding. There was a lot of water under her quarterdeck, which was giving her a considerable list to port. Her stern was well down, the portholes were half submerged and the Admiral's gallery partly underwater. TRADESMAN was the first of the two tugs to arrive. She put a line on WARSPITE's bow and began pulling out to starboard. MASTERMAN was fast to her stern soon afterwards and hauled to port. Once the initial inertia was overcome WARSPITE swung with surprising rapidity. At one time she was nearly stern on to the Mount. Then the tugs changed over. TRADESMAN pulled the bows to port towards the Mount and MASTERMAN pulled her stern to starboard away from it. This corrected the swing, but the momentum soon carried her the other way and a reverse correction had to be made. The ding-dong battle went on for two hours and at 6 pm it was decided she could not effectively be moved further. All the salvage chiefs went aboard. Mr Bauer said that owing to the danger of working in darkness close to the rocks this morning's early tide will probably not be used but the tugs would try her again on Saturday night. [28]

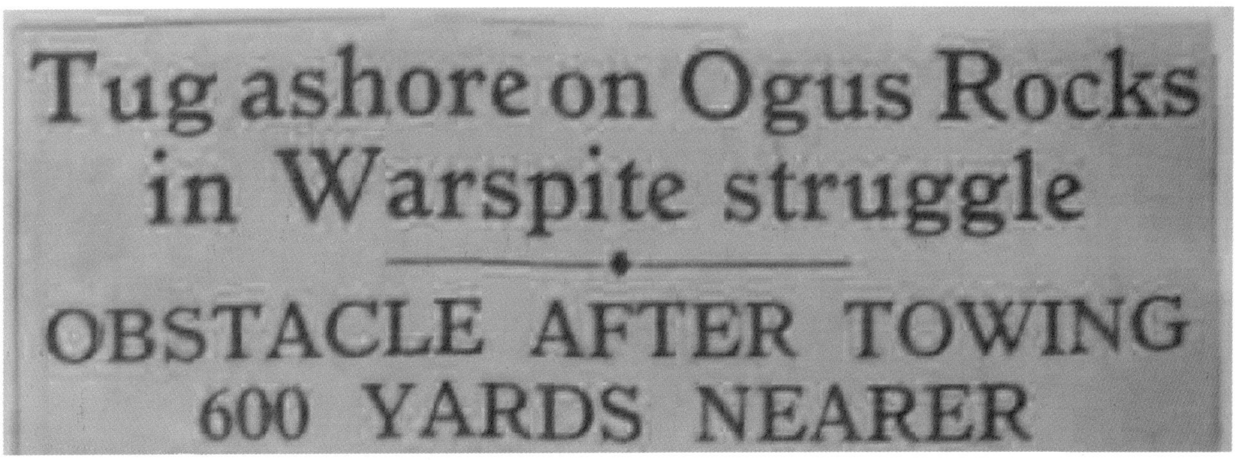
Tug ashore on Ogus Rocks in Warspite struggle

OBSTACLE AFTER TOWING 600 YARDS NEARER

[28] Western Morning News 11 December 1950.

Following this adventure, the crew of MASTERMAN had to be rescued by the reserve Penlee lifeboat M.O.Y.E which towed the unfortunate tug into Newlyn. She was subsequently repaired in Hull.

MASTERMAN in dry dock at Hull repairing damage from her grounding on Hogus Rocks.
United Towing Society

The adverse winter weather was causing problems, as it did throughout WARSPITE's time in Cornwall, as noted in November 1950:

During recent rough weather a move was attempted but the vessel is now in a worse position than at Marazion beach; a large part of the vessel has been awash and there has been extensive damage to electrical gear.

WMC were becoming frustrated with Bauer's efforts and had been looking at alternatives for their WARSPITE investment. Clyde shipbreakers, Arnott Young had just broken up WARSPITE's sisters HMS QUEEN ELIZABETH and HMS VALIANT and were invited to visit Cornwall by WMC in September 1950. However, they felt they could not help with the demolition or acquire WARSPITE. It is interesting that Arnott Young, as one of the UK's leading four shipbreakers, felt the WARSPITE hulk was too much of a challenge for them. WMC ploughed on regardless, perhaps they had little alternative, beyond abandoning the hulk, but had invested huge amounts in the project with little return to date. There was concern from engineer Duncan Nicholson in September 1950 in a report to WMC as to what Bauer was doing with the ship:

It would appear that Bauer is digging in his toes for the winter. New hands continue to make their appearance and the compartments under the Admiral's quarters are being prepared with countless man hours as living quarters. There is now quite a lot of talk of taking off the side armour, turrets etc and taking away the lightened vessel next summer. Looks like they intend to hang this job out, goodness knows. Regarding the equipment he brought down at the start of the job, it was roughly as follows... 30 Ford8 3-inch fire pumps, these were in a useless state, nearly all had carburettors, magnetos or both missing. Out of all that lot we only got two working and these were never used ... goodness knows what is to be done with the WARSPITE, I sometimes wonder if she will ever be broken up.

The project was struggling. Friction continued to worsen between WMC and their Bauer contractors, as a non-executive director of WMC commented in November 1950.

I know that as from 18th November we are no longer paying out any money unless it is in order to get non-ferrous metal in return. Nevertheless, we continue presumably to be legally liable for any trespass or other crimes which may be committed on our behalf by Bauer.

In March 1951 WMC complained that Bauer had diverted some of the WARSPITE workforce to another salvage project, a 'ferry job', a possible salvage of the wrecked King Harry ferry.

There were disputes about over charging by Bauer on their cost returns. The Bauer agreement enabling Bauer to charge actual costs plus 5% as well as taking a proportion of profit. However, did all the recharged costs relate to WARSPITE? In May 1951, solicitors for Bauer complained though that their clients had not been paid for three months. Later WMC commented that at one stage they had spent an astonishing £120,000 to date on the WARSPITE project.

Hitherto the ship's own seaplane crane had been used to lift scrap around and off the ship. But it was fixed and capacity was limited to ten tons. However, in March 1951 an 'Electric Lorrain' mobile crane was leased and came into operation. This could lift 22 tons and was to improve efficiency considerably as it could lift slabs of armour plate, which had been 'unbolted' from the hull and allowed to fall on to the seabed. These would then usually be cut in two to facilitate transportation to shore on lighters and unloading on the quay at Penzance by a P and H crane. In March 1951, work started on cutting up the barbettes, remunerative work potentially but not an easy task as they were thickly armoured. 400 tons of steel from the deck was taken also: the first significant scrap sale from the ship for two years.

Lorrain crane lifting armour plate.
Walsall

Quite often a shipbreaker will sell equipment from a ship for reuse. This was rare in the case of WARSPITE but a gear wheel from the ship was reground and exhibited at the British Industries Fair at Castle Bromwich in Spring 1951[29].

[29] Coventry Evening Telegraph 28 April 1951.

In November 1951 BISCO agreed to pay fortnightly for scrap (rather than their usual monthly terms) to help WMC deal with "heavy wage bills". Clearly cash flow was an issue. In February 1952, discussions were to take place with BISCO as to the prices they would pay for steel. BISCO were unhappy with 'very disappointing deliveries', although they understood the bad winter weather had not helped. However, in recognition of the difficulties that WMC faced in operating offshore, BISCO were unusually paying considerably more for WARSPITE steel than the controlled steel scrap price, then dictated by central government.

A somewhat chaotic situation is confirmed by another memorandum from engineer Duncan Nicholson to WMC in December 1951, Nicholson is extremely concerned at the state of play on Bauer's breaking up the wreck. There is a need to refloat her to bring her in closer to shore to break up, and yet this process would mean less short-term financial return as extraction of metals would need to be deferred. Nicholson suggests removing 2500 tons of armour with the dual purpose of producing a monetary return and to lighten the hulk, making refloating easier in consequence. He reports that the valuable non-ferrous metal is generally in inaccessible flooded parts of the ship and talks of the weekly wage bill having fallen to just £100. Unbeknown perhaps to him, management accounts for the 6 months to 31 December 1951 show a slender profit of £880 and arrears of payments to Bauer of £4013. Although 2,518 tons of steel had been extracted in the previous six months, only 15 tons of the much more valuable non-ferrous had been taken.

Low tide view looking from Marazion with the hulk to the west of the Mount. *Author's collection*

WMC's relationship with Bauer had deteriorated even further by late 1951 with reports of Bauer taking away from Cornwall, plant and equipment belonging to WMC. Also, Bauer senior staff were allegedly not cooperating with the workforce or anyone from WMC. With the Bauer contract expiring in late January 1952, WMC decided not to renew the arrangement and were prepared to evict Bauer management from the wreck at midnight on the relevant day, should this be necessary. There was concern that further key pieces of plant might be taken away by Bauer. WMC had taken legal advice:

(Counsel) again warns that we must not interfere in the operations of recovering steel or indeed of any operations on the vessel, but we are of course entitled to take reasonable steps to protect our own property where it is in a very obvious danger of being abused.

Bauer withdrew without any trouble and ceased to be involved in the WARSPITE project. Two other local salvage companies, (Metcalfe Marine Salvage and Penzance Shippers and Salvage) offered their services to WMC[30] but WMC decided to directly employ most of the workforce, previously working for Bauer. The WMC team was managed by two senior employees, the 'two Macs' – Neil Macdonald and Neil MacQuarrie they had been involved from an early stage and been salvage managers under Bauer. Besides their wage, they negotiated incentivised payments based on tonnage extracted; perhaps 75p per ton for ferrous and £5 for non-ferrous. A bonus would be paid if the project finished early. The Macs were just 31 and 27 respectively at the time they took over as the main figures managing the project day to day. Frank Wilson was in overall charge as WMC's new Penzance representative, making frequent visits and then buying a house nearby. Duncan Nicholson, the engineer involved since 1947, made up the management panel of four.

The 'Two Macs' Neil Macdonald (left) and Neil MacQuarrie. *I MacQuarrie collection*

Scrap cut from WARSPITE was normally landed on the Albert Pier at Penzance by a variety of craft, including the EMPEROR and barges towed by the CHEW MAGNA, a 52.5-foot ex Admiralty Harbour Launch Diesel (HLD): the steel scrap was then loaded on to railway wagons to be taken, normally to Sheffield, but sometimes other destinations, such as South Wales. A P & H crane was purchased for this important task. On occasions scrap spilled out of the wagons or they broke down, delaying their arrival in Sheffield. It seems the rail company provided somewhat decrepit wagons on occasions. Non-ferrous scrap was taken by lorry to

[30] In May 1954, WMC acquired the latter company for unknown reasons. (WMC letter to BISCO 14 July 1954, Walsall.)

WMC's base at Wednesfield, near Wolverhampton. The journey was hard, taking two days and two nights and the lorries had no power steering, let alone heating. Sea transport was also used on occasions. In late 1952, the coaster ALBATROS carrying £5,546 worth of WARSPITE scrap (including 167 tons of armour plate) sank off the Isle of Wight, en route to Hull, thankfully the insurance company paid up for this.

Around this time, a policeman rang up one day to report that WARSPITE had apparently disappeared: the hulk had sunk into the sand and becoming covered. Sand was a problem for the demolition crew and at a later stage, sometimes up to three feet would need to be dug out before work could start. It was unsurprising that on occasions, steel mills would complain of the mud and sand in scrap sent to them from WARSPITE.

From time to time, there were protests from St Aubyn Estates on St Michael's Mount about alleged damage to their harbour wall and silting caused by WARSPITE's proximity. When the Duke of Kent visited in January 1948, a party from St Michael's Mount had been given a tour of WARSPITE, then still at Prussia Cove, see images on next page. Their expressions possibly hint at displeasure at being caught on camera.

An undated view of the hulk from St Michael's Mount, maybe 1952. *Penlee*

Left: Giles St Aubyn, a young Duke of Kent, Lord St Levan, and manager Ted Penrose on board. Right: A workman possibly Bennett, Lord St Levan, the Duke of Kent and Giles St Aubyn[31] aboard WARSPITE whilst still at Prussia Cove January 1948. *Penlee*

The project's efficiency improved dramatically in April 1952 when the Royal Aircraft Establishment at Farnborough lent two Rolls Royce Derwent Mk 5 aero gas turbines to pump compressed air into the ship's compartments. (Press reports refer to them incorrectly as jet engines on occasions.) The gas turbines took less than two hours to float the ship. Hitherto the twenty-seven air compressors had taken at least two days to do this and were prone to overheating and consequential breakdown. However, the gas turbines were quite costly to operate, using 500 gallons of paraffin each hour. Bauer had experimented with the gas turbines in late 1951.

The hulk on 5 May 1952, well cut down. Bulges by the stern have been removed, leaving the gaps in the side. The starboard hanger continues to be used as an equipment store and a shelter for the workforce in bad weather. *Topfoto*

[31] 3rd Lord St Levan (1895-1978). Giles St Aubyn.(1925-2015) taught History at Eton and became a famous author. In 1948 he was giving some tuition to the Duke of Kent (1935-).

The gas turbines being started on 12 May 1952. *Rolls-Royce*

The turbines were first used on 5 May 1952, with the Rolls Royce team initially comprising Messrs Tunnicliffe, Wilson and Jordan pictured below (image courtesy of Rolls-Royce plc) were the initial Rolls Royce specialists deployed.

Rolls-Royce

Rolls-Royce

WARSPITE being quickly refloated, using the gas turbines, and guided towards shore by two hawsers, one on the Chapel Rock onshore and another secured to a rock on the Mount.

Rolls-Royce

However, on this occasion a pump failed, and the ship unfortunately only moved forty feet nearer the shore.

The 30,000-ton battleship, which two years ago defied the efforts of powerful tugs to move her from the rocks and on which she had settled alongside St Michaels Mount, yesterday moved herself nearer to the shore. Buoyed up by compressed air pumped into her by jet engines, being used for the first time in the salvage, she lifted herself once again from the seabed and using her own winches pulled herself towards the beach by wire ropes attached to the rocks on the shore. By continued efforts through the week, it is hoped to move her 600 feet, but she is only movable at the peak of the tide, a period measured in minutes. Yesterday she moved 30 feet. She would probably have done more but one of the powerful pumps on board refused to start, so that she had not full buoyancy. Mr F.H. Wilson a director of the Wolverhampton Metal Company said that the company proposed to move the hulk by successive stages until she was so high up the beach that she was left high and dry at low tide so that she could be cut up completely. "That cannot be achieved this year" he said "when we have got her as far as we can this week, we shall continue to take metal from her and later in the summer we shall float her again and try to bring her still further in." One wire goes ashore to a rock on the Mount from a winch at the forward end of the superstructure. Another wire pays out over the quarter deck, and it's made fast to the Chapel Rock at the shore end of the causeway to the Mount. By heaving in gently on these two lines the shippers move slowly near to the shore as she floats.[32]

The gas turbines were used over fifty times until January 1956 to refloat the ship or in tests and adjustments. The image on left shows a slit cut through the Chapel Rock at Marazion quite possibly used for the hawser out to WARSPITE. However, it is understood that shortly after the refloating on May 5, 1952, the wire to Chapel Rock snapped and was not set up again for use. Later in December 1952, the Birmingham Post reported at length on the state of play:

On the Cornish Riviera, hard by the old Priory topped island of St Michael's Mount, near Penzance the winter seas are chafing a half-dismantled steel hulk which is all that remains of the battleship WARSPITE. Two hundred and fifty miles away, her owners – no longer the lordships of the Admiralty, but the Wolverhampton Metal Company

[32] Western Morning News 6 May 1952.

of Wednesfield – are tackling the problem of completing the salvage of the vessel, which is lying with a broken back 900 yards offshore, in 45 feet of water. One first sees the WARSPITE as the train to Penzance swings suddenly alongside Mount's Bay, and St Michaels Mount rises above the railway sidings and sand dunes. The ship is in the shape of a shallow "V" – no longer an inverted one. Nothing remains of her upper works except the aircraft hangar amidships which now protects a large crane – taken to the ship in sections and assembled on deck. Lately it has been swinging the 22-ton armour plates into the lighter. There are two smaller cranes fore and aft. I cross to St Michael's Mount on the causeway that is exposed on low tide and climb the wall of the little harbour to get a closer view of the WARSPITE 100 yards away. Time and weather had variously coloured her once grey sides. She was pink amidships and dark green at the waterline, shading down to black below. The bows were deep red with rust. The aircraft hangar bore streamers of frayed paint and metal, like wallpaper crumbling from the walls of a deserted house. The torpedo bulges have been removed from the side, leaving the bulkheads protruding like ribs. A red launch was alongside and a crane, its diesel engine puffing and smoking was dragging a large piece of armour plate from the seabed. From the ship's vitals came the sound of hammers.

The Admiral's walk still encircles the stern, an incongruous remnant of dignity. The fracture was clearly visible – a wedge shaped crack just above the low tide water level. Under a grey sky a grey green sea lapped gently amid the rocks. Salvage work is conducted from WARSPITE office, Marazion – a little boarded off cubicle in a sea front garage. On the wall is a vast Admiralty plan of the WARSPITE with all the compartments numbered. The lighters and 'Duck' ply back and forth to the ship, which one can see close at hand through the office window.

Close by St Michael's Mount in this undated view, perhaps 1952. There were claims that the hulk was damaging the harbour wall and silting up the entrance. *Author's collection*

The seafaring folk of Penzance, Marazion and Newlyn sympathise with the WARSPITE in her fallen state. "It's no end for a ship", one of them said to me, amid smells of fish and diesel oil at Newlyn. One shares that sympathy for a fine and gallant vessel but there is no consolation in the thought that the WARSPITE which bravely defended our country in two world wars, is sacrificing herself to help Britain's economic recovery.[33]

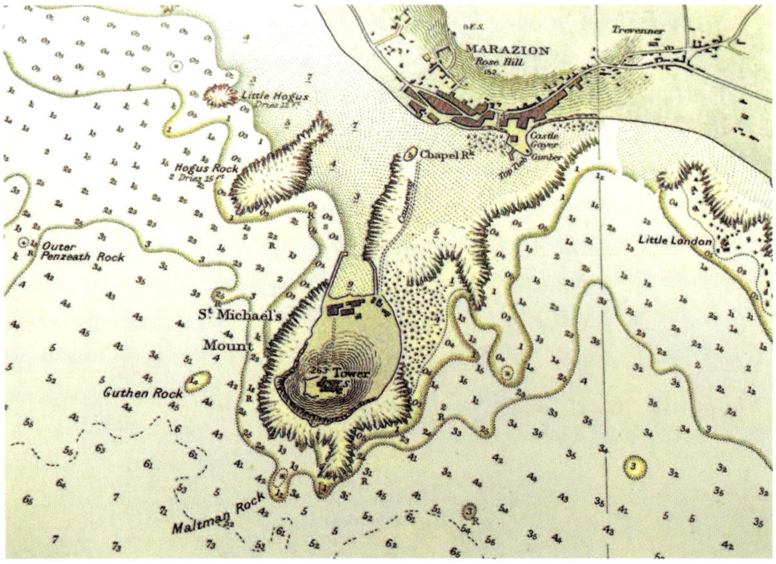

Extract from Admiralty chart OCB777 of the area around St Michael's Mount, the ship was moved around the area to the left/west of the Mount. A hawser was tied to the Chapel Rock and the Hogus Rock also features in the story.
UK Hydrographic Office

Starboard hangar and seaplane crane still intact 9 May 1952. *Rolls-Royce*

[33] Birmingham Post 30 December 1952

Two views of the hulk on 9 May 1952. Above: looking forward towards bows. Below seen from the water.
Rolls-Royce

CHAPTER 5

CUT IN HALF AND THE FINAL DAYS 1953-1956

In early 1953, WMC became especially mindful of the crack which had nearly severed the hull. This crack had arisen in the early days at Prussia Cove. In the undated image below, the two Macs are examining it. In anticipation of the hulk being cut into two sections, WMC arranged for several surveys being undertaken.

Walsall

In February 1953, marine consultants Harold B. Mylchreest reviewed the bow section. A month earlier, some Falmouth naval architects had been engaged. In April 1953, Captain Noble of E.W. Nicholls visited.

The two halves of WARSPITE had caused issues since her back was broken at Prussia Cove. Even though the two sections had not quite been severed, in March 1953, BISCO offered £85,000 for the bow section. This was reckoned to weigh 10,000 tons, including maybe 150 tons of non-ferrous. BISCO required WMC to get the section towed to South Wales, arriving with no more than a 25-foot draught. It was planned to break this section up at Oxwich Bay or near Mumbles – in each case, the demolition could only have been carried out on the beach. Quite extraordinary but not a fantasy; BISCO was a substantial organisation, owned by the British steel industry which was short of scrap. BISCO sensibly protected their position by making the actual purchase price, dependent on the actual metal recovered. In the end insurance cover for the tow proved prohibitive, so the sale fell through.

A diver with colleagues.
K. Babbage collection

There had been earlier, more speculative offers for the wreck. Back in February 1950 with the ship still on the rocks at Prussia Cove, agents for Italian shipbreakers made a high bid of £150,000 for the hulk. However, this was on the optimistic basis that there was still 20,000 tons of steel, 5,000 tons of armour and 1,000 tons of non-ferrous still to be extracted from WARSPITE. The bid was rejected. In September 1950, agents for a Victor White offered a derisory £30,000 for the hulk. However, such was WMC's concern at the state of the project at that time, that it was only rejected after Board discussion.

Another approach was made in January 1953 by an agent for possible Italian buyers, asking what price was required by WMC and querying whether the hulk could be towed to Genoa for break up, an unlikely prospect!

On 24 April 1953, the two parts were finally severed by diver Jim Craig and pulled apart by hawser. A newspaper article joked that each section had its own captain and crew. In fact, the bow and stern sections were somewhat different in size. WARSPITE had been 640 feet in length and the front severed section was just 264 feet in length, 100 foot in width and a depth of 38 feet. The ship was split in two at frames 100 to 110; so not a straight cut across.

The two halves were kept close together possibly as the cranes on the stern section were needed to work on the bow part, particularly the heavy armour plate located there. There were twenty-ton slabs of armour that were held by seven bolts on to the hull. The bolts were loosened, and the slabs fell to the sea bottom. A diver located them there and then a crane would lift them out on to the deck for cutting.

Left: **WARSPITE** twisted but not quite yet cut in half March 1953. Right: The great ship cut in half, the two parts just 30 feet apart. Walsall

The bow section was moved closer to the shore to the shallower water and in May 1953, for example, it was pulled 40 feet nearer the beach by hawser. This enabled demolition to be conducted much more easily, leading to swifter extraction of metals.

STRANDED ON ROCK IN 60 m.p.h. GALE

Men saved after 3-hour ordeal

Amphibious, ex-military, DUKW vehicles were used to ferry the workforce out to WARSPITE, see appendix 4.6 for an evocative newsreel film depicting this. In February 1954, Bill Brewer (appendix 6.3) was stranded on the Hogus Rock with the two Macs after his DUKW's engine broke down, due to contaminated petrol, from an unknown source. The Hogus Rock is covered at high tide and fortunately they were spotted from St Michael's Mount and the alarm raised. A boat came out to rescue them and had to throw a line to the three men with a lifebelt attached, as it could not get close to the Rock.

A DUKW on the beach at Marazion c1952. *S. Trudgen collection*

By March 1954, the bow section was just 700 feet from the high-water mark, compared to the ship being 2700 feet out in December 1952. Progress!

The starboard seaplane hangar was a major feature of WARSPITE until a very late stage in the demolition. The image below shows how the interior was used for the storage of plant - compressors and generators here. Workers could also shelter there in adverse weather conditions!

I. MacQuarrie collection

The ship cut in half with St Michael's Mount. *S. Trudgen collection*

Undated image of the two halves of the great ship. *MTSC*

In September 1954, WMC reported good progress:

Due to the excellent work of our personnel at Penzance, substantial tonnages of steel and non-ferrous metal have been recovered and sold or in the case of, non-ferrous metal, used in our production. The proceeds from these recoveries particularly on the non-ferrous side have steadily reduced our outlay. The improved progress of this venture resulted mainly from the cutting of the vessel into two sections. This major operation, involving underwater cutting, was successful thanks for the skill of a diver and engineers and enabled us to pull both fore and aft sections practically onto the beach. A part of the fore end is actually clear of the water at low tide. Having regard to the further expected recoveries we are hopeful that subject to there being no unforeseen setbacks, the venture will ultimately prove successful.[34]

The two halves of the hull under St. Michael's Mount.
S. Trudgen collection

[34] Financial Times 15 September, 1954

Boiler room April 1954; a shaky looking ladder. *I. MacQuarrie collection*

By April 1955, the bow section had been demolished, leaving the more substantial stern section, some way offshore, to cut up.

The still elegant, if weather-beaten, stern with Admiral's walkway intact.

I. MacQuarrie collection

In arguing for better prices for their steel from this, WMC may have exaggerated the practical difficulties to BISCO:

Our main problem at the moment is whether we can economically salvage the remaining half which is some distance from the shore when we have suffered considerable setback as a result of the winter gales and exceptionally hard weather during recent months. The economics have changed considerably as we reach the final stages, and it remains for decision as to how far the recovery can be pursued, particularly as regards recovering the steel from the keel and lower portions, much of which is submerged in sand.

Fire is a constant hazard to any shipbreaker and in March 1956, for example, thick smoke rose from the aft section, caused by the igniting of oil on deck. The workers were evacuated for a while and some equipment was damaged.

The hulk close to the beach.
Author's collection

Stern out of the water at low tide, revealing propeller shafts. *K. Macdonald collection*

Neil Macdonald (right) in turbine area of the ship on 3 September 1955 with two other workers. One of the 12-inch pumps and suction tubes can also be seen. *Walsall*

The successful WMC team; the Macs (left), Frank Wilson and diver Jim Craig. *Walsall*

By July 1956, only 600 tons of the hulk remained to be dismantled. In August 1956, it was noted that two boilers (50 tons) would be blown up as it would not be cost effective to dismantle them for scrap. Their remnants can still be seen by divers. Discussions took place as to disposal of the plant used in the project, now at its end. The Macs acquired some of it for use in the MacSalvors business that they subsequently set up. The P & H crane (appendix 6.2 shows an image) was particularly useful.

Finally on 21 August 1956, the remnants of WARSPITE finally disappeared, as reported in the Birmingham Post:

The wreck of the 30,000-ton battleship WARSPITE which has been a diminishing landmark in the sea near St Michael's Mount Cornwall disappeared forever yesterday when salvage men, in three hours, remove the last 60 tons from the sands. About 25,000 tons of scrap have been removed, including 5000 tons of armour plating. Mr Neil Macdonald, one of the salvage directors, said yesterday "It has been a hard struggle. It was really too big to start demolitions here. There have been accidents and one fatality. I'm very glad to see the end of it now".

How successful was the WARSPITE project? No doubt an amazing act of salvage from Prussia Cove and great work by the team on demolition. Financially WMC reported a profit of £35,000 to their shareholders. Under the headline *'Battleship Gamble makes a profit'* the Daily Express reported this profit in July 1956. Indeed, it was something of a gamble and T.C. James, managing director of WMC revealed though that WMC had once been '£120,000 down on the deal'. He credited a boom in scrap metal prices, (four or five times higher than when WMC bought WARSPITE) for the profit achieved. Another later press report in 1957 stated that their profit on WARSPITE had been higher, at £52,000. The success of the venture is confirmed by WMC relieving Brewis, one of the Bristol scrap merchants, of a debt of £2750 as a gesture of goodwill and as promised if the WARSPITE venture was successful. Not a huge financial return overall for WMC given the risk and enormous effort put in but at least a profit. The financial side of the project is considered in more detail in Appendix 2.

CHAPTER 6

CONCLUSIONS

Memories of WARSPITE are still strong in West Cornwall and it's an interesting story. Many locals are proud that family members worked on the wreck or can remember the giant hulk out in Mount's Bay as it was gradually dismembered. An 'ever present' for many in their childhood.

The appearance of the great ship has been likened to the washed up 'drowned giant' on a beach appearing suddenly in J.G. Ballard's novel and film of the same name[35].

Were it not for the storm of 22 and 23 April 1947, WARSPITE would no doubt have been recycled efficiently by MI at Faslane. An experienced team of around 50 workers would have cut her down, deck by deck, with little fuss and she would have ceased to exist by late 1948.

Some recognition for the great ship's service while in commission. *Author's collection*

As it was, it took over three years for WARSPITE just to be patched up and refloated, albeit in an amazing act of salvage. However, in the meantime her superstructure, funnel and turrets had been removed also, helping to pay substantial costs. It was a long project as after being towed along the coast in 1950 to Marazion a few miles, she took another six years to finish off.

WMC, a listed company, had a prominent role throughout. First, they subsidised the Bristol scrap merchants in buying the wreck in 1947 and then

[35] *The Drowned Giant* – J.G Ballard. A short particularly good film version can be found on Netflix 'Love, Death, and Robots' series.

bought it from them in 1949. WMC's next 'partner' Bauer believed that the wreck could be refloated and scrapped profitably, particularly as metal prices were increasing fast. All quite an adventure with rather more financial risk than a quoted company might normally take.

There have been few other occasions when a substantial ship has been bought not by shipbreakers but by large metal trader companies who necessarily delegated demolition work to contractors. The large aircraft carriers EAGLE and ARK ROYAL in 1978 and 1980 were other examples. In the latter, the contractors' performance was lamentable. WMC's experience was much better.

The alliance with Bauer enabled the refloating, one of the greatest acts of salvage ever undertaken in the UK. The ship had been sunk offshore and some of her bottom torn out, lingering at Prussia Cove for more than three years. For the final six years, the hulk was moved closer and closer to the shore under a successful management team of the Macs who were to demonstrate later their business acumen by setting up the still successful Cornish business MacSalvors. Steel was sold at a particularly high price in recognition by the UK steel industry's BISCO of the difficult conditions offshore. The price might also have reflected the lack of shipbreaking scrap as few other large naval ships were broken up (at least between 1951 and 1955) at a time of war in Korea.

For virtually all the period from 1947 to 1956, it should be remembered that the hulk of WARSPITE was not even afloat but filled to a large extent with water and on the sea floor. The ultimate success was down to increasing non-ferrous scrap prices, strong direction and leadership and a loyal and hardworking workforce. They got the job done despite awful winter weather and with a ship underwater for much of the time!

CHAPTER 7

WARSPITE TODAY

Very little indeed of the original WARSPITE ship survives offshore, although parts of the boilers are visible to divers by St Michael's Mount. The Wreck card of the UK Hydrographic Office refers to various dives to check their condition and on 28 December 2000, for example, it was noted these covered an area 30 metres long, 12 metres wide and 7.4 metres high[36] and comprised:

'Two huge vertical boilers from the main part of the wreck, with hull plating and scattered debris in between.'

There is also metal on the seabed at Prussia Cove. However, when any ship is recycled, some of the constituent parts may be extracted either for commercial use or as mementoes. Many such items survive from WARSPITE.

Two views of the piece of armour on display in Pool, near Redruth.

The largest 'onshore' relic, by some way, is a piece of armour, now on display outside MacSalvors premises, at Pool, Redruth, which is thought to weigh six tons. Found buried in the sand at Prussia Cove c1990, its history is unclear. It has not been cut off by the breakers' torches, but possibly blown off by enemy action during World War 2 and kept onboard. It is quite possibly from a barbette given its curved shape. The MacSalvors business was

[36] Other reports from the wreck card show smaller areas of wreckage.

founded by the two Macs in 1957 after completion of their work on WARSPITE. Many workers on WARSPITE continued to work for MacSalvors, some for long periods such as crane manager Henry Payne, working for 35 years. MacSalvors continues to be a major successful business in Cornwall, with crane depots or outlets in Plymouth, Truro, Bodmin, Redruth and Penryn. It is still owned by the two Macs' families and managed by two of Neil MacQuarrie's sons Cameron and Iain. Their impressive website shows the wide range of their activities. Initially the business dealt in Ministry of Defence surplus and was engaged in dismantling and demolition work. Hundreds of factory clearances have been completed. In 1962 a crane hire division was established, and plant was supplied for major projects in the West Country such as the Goonhilly earth satellite station and widening of the Tamar Bridge. An extraordinarily wide range of goods is still dealt in as well as the core retail and plant hire activities.

At another location, which remains confidential, a spar and derrick survive from WARSPITE, happily there are plans for them to be restored.

The impressive Marazion Museum has a very interesting WARSPITE room with many artefacts. The stern post (right) is particularly impressive as is a superb builder's model of WARSPITE in her original form, upon completion in 1915.

The post, which acted as an anchor for the Blondin wire, still survives in situ at Prussia Cove. It is almost certainly part of the topmast from WARSPITE.

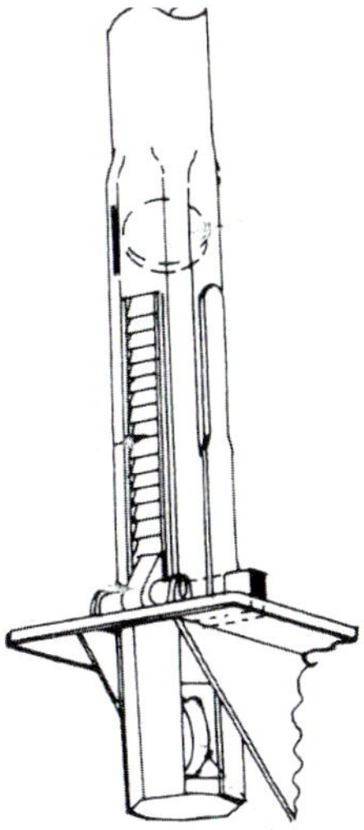

Far left: The post today.

Left: A diagram by the late Captain G Hogg.

Below: An image from February 1949 shows the post when the Blondin wire was in operation.
M. Crowdy/WSPL

On far left are a clock and barometer and on right, some drawers reputedly from the bunk in the captain's cabin. All retained at the Marazion Hotel.

After the Fritz 1 glider bomb hit in 1943, WARSPITE was patched up and ballasted with concrete. One of the surviving concrete blocks is shown here below. Concrete had no value to any shipbreaker and there are costs and delays involved in taking it out of any hulk.

WARSPITE was built with 150 or so tons of teak and much of this was recycled as flooring. A good example is at the Greenbank Hotel, Falmouth, shown above. It is sad to relate that much teak was burnt as a home could not be found for it. More WARSPITE teak can be found at the Cornish Choughs pub in Camborne. It was also used for garden seats, the Maypole Garden in Marazion, is just one of many examples.

Teak was also recycled usefully to make relics and ornaments, examples of which on display at Marazion Museum are shown above.

Shown on the left are a bronze woodpecker badge from the Admiral's Quarters and two bottom heavy swivel chairs from the officers' mess, guaranteed not to fall over, even in the wildest seas.

Author's collection

A treadplate (above) and companionway (below left) from the WARSPITE are pictured. More utilitarian items can be reused, including portholes. Portholes (bottom right).

A diver's helmet and boots believed to have been used in operations on WARSPITE, are shown on right. The ship's bell was removed by a Mr R. Morris (another bidder for the wreck) at the behest of the ultimate purchaser Bennett and taken to Penzance for safekeeping. Reputedly it ended up at the offices of WMC at Wednesfield and when these were demolished in the early 1990s, it was lost. But the bell is now held by the Imperial War Museum in London.

Author's collection

The WARSPITE name lives on in four particular ways:

- a nuclear submarine which entered service in 1967 but laid up at Devonport since 1991, still awaiting disposal in 2023.
- In 2019 moreover, it was announced that the third next generation nuclear deterrent submarine would be called WARSPITE. She will enter service in the 2030s.
- In 2021, a new housing development in Marazion included a Warspite Way.
- A memorial erected by the HMS Warspite Association, unveiled in 1992 on the seafront at Marazion.

K. Stewart

SOURCE MATERIAL AND ACKNOWLEDGMENTS

Primary

- The WARSPITE files of WMC, kept at the Walsall Library and Local History Centre, proved extremely useful. (For referencing in this text 'Walsall' has been used.)
- The transcript of a BBC Radio programme 'The End of the Old Lady', broadcast in 1957, featured most of the main players in the WARSPITE project in Cornwall 1947/56. Referred to as 'BBC 1957 Radio Programme' in the text and found on WMC files at Walsall.
- Reports of WARSPITE in Cornwall frequently appeared in both national and local press. Reports are usually detailed and evocative and usefully dated.
- MI minutes and other papers at MTSC for details of their involvement with WARSPITE.
- The Newlyn Archive provided very helpful copy papers of meetings in September 1950 on WARSPITE's possible move to sites at or near Newlyn.
- Discussions with last survivor of WARSPITE workforce, Bill Brewer in 2022/3.
- UK Hydrographic Office for Admiralty Charts and Wreck notes.
- Some evocative newsreel films, as listed in Appendix 4.

Secondary

- 'WARSPITE – *an eventful end to a fine career'* – Fred George, Warship World 1986, p12/3.
- *'The Life of a Boat'* – Graeme Ewens (BukuPress,2021) – history of the *W and S* lifeboat.
- Iain MacQuarrie with recollections of his father Neil's involvement and tireless in supplying extensive source material.
- Dr Ian Buxton, leading shipbreaking expert and behind creation of the MTSC.
- Peter Tunstall-Behrens, owner of land at Prussia Cove.
- Marazion Museum – a very interesting Warspite room.
- Darrell Jago, Janet Wilce, members of the Nicholson family and many other relatives of Warspite workers. Syd Trudgen
- HMS Warspite Association
- Neil Chattle of the Rolls Royce Heritage Trust.
- Elaine Bawden, press officer for the Penlee Lifeboat
- Ian Watson, MD of the last major UK shipbreaker, Shipbreaking Queenborough
- Maritime historians including Philip Simons, Brian Hargreaves Jonathan Griffin, Anthony Holtham, and others such as David Fricker, Michael Noonan, Peter Bass, Mike Critchley, Dave Sowdon, Steve Tacey and David Asprey.
- Penlee House and Gallery, Penzance for photos. ('Penlee' in caption credits)
- Rona Goodwin, Andy Gardner, and Mike Hawkins.
- Support from J & AR, MB, JDL, RFJ & GJ and Artwrite Hythe.
- Last, but not least, Belinda Body and her team at the Cornwall Heritage Trust and Krispen Atkinson and Dennis Maccoy of the World Ship Society.

APPENDIX 1 – WARSPITE: TIMELINE OF KEY EVENTS

20 April 1947	Leaves Spithead bound for Faslane.
23 April 1947	Wrecked at Prussia Cove
August 1947	Bought by Bristol scrap merchants Bennett and Brewis for £25,000.
November 1947	Bennett and Brewis transfer wreck to Western Salvaging Co Ltd (WSL).
May 1949	WMC acquire wreck from WSL.
18 July 1949	Salvage contractors Bauer engaged by WMC to deal with wreck.
15 March 1950	Accident leading to death of John Lennie MacQuarrie
29 July 1950	Refloated at Prussia Cove and towed to Marazion by tugs.
May 1951	A move leads to ship breaking her back.
25 January 1952	WMC choose not to renew Bauer contract. The 'Macs' subsequently manage the project – Neil Macdonald and Neil MacQuarrie.
5 May 1952	First use of gas turbines to facilitate refloating.
26 March 1953	BISCO offer to buy front half for £85,000.
24 April 1953	Two parts of ship finally severed by diver.
May 1955	Demolition of bow section completed.
21 August 1956	Last scrap lifted from wreck.
29 April 1957	Macs form MacSalvors Ltd, using some plant used in WARSPITE project.
4 August 1957	BBC radio broadcast a 30-minute production on WARSPITE in Cornwall

APPENDIX 2 – FINANCIAL ISSUES

2.1 Introduction

Shipbreakers will look to recycle as much as possible of a ship they buy for demolition. Appendix 7 below shows the detailed criteria that original purchasers, Metal Industries (MI) adopted in costing their bid for the ship. They knew from experience that any ship would contain rubbish, such as concrete (usually there to provide ballast) and harmful material such as asbestos. What would be left would comprise broadly steel, valuable non-ferrous metals (e.g., copper) and equipment that might be sold for re use. The shipbreaker would need to estimate what sale prices might ultimately be obtained for all of these. Prices fluctuate depending on market conditions, although in the period under review here, they generally increased sharply. Beyond the purchase price of the ship (and associated towage and insurance), the main costs would relate to the premises (e.g., rent), labour and oxygen. Each purchaser of WARSPITE is now reviewed in the light of these principles.

2.2 MI

MI were long established and one of the UK's two major shipbreakers, keeping careful records of materials extracted from their ships. Their estimates of both quantity and likely value of scrap on WARSPITE were based on a thorough review of the ship and the outturn from broadly similar ships they had scrapped in the 1930s. They had carried out an inspection of WARSPITE in September . However, in the absence of any special deal with steel mills or with BISCO, MI would have been bound by the 'controlled steel scrap price' which at the time was just £3.40/ton and this is reflected in their figures below which is based on their first estimate (July 1946), set out in Appendix 7. They did not know, when doing this estimate, that the 15-inch gun barrels would be removed prior to break up and these would have reduced outturn by say 800 of the expected 1,200 tons of steel from the ship's guns, to the following figures.

	Tons	**Per ton (£)**	**Yield £'000**
Steel	12,340	*3.40*	*42*
Nickel chrome	6,000	*5*	*30*
Armour	2,000	*3.40*	*7*
Cast iron	500	*4.40*	*2*
Boiler tubes	400	*16*	*6*
Non-ferrous	1,025	*53*	*54*
Lead/zinc	100	*30*	*3*
Gun scrap	300	*3*	*1*
Sundry	1,235		*7*
Totals	**23,800**		*152*

A slight reduction in the expected gross revenue therefore to £152,000. MI were experienced in calculating outturns so their weight estimates should be treated with respect, but they look cautious as subsequently on their own demolition, WARSPITE'S three sister ships, albeit not all as fully modernised, gave rise to 11%-13% more metal (see table in Appendix 2.4 below).

MI acquired WARSPITE for £101,275 in April 1947 so a reasonable profit was anticipated, even after allowing for towage, insurance, and labour costs. The insurance proceeds of £147,250 (net of commission) meant that even after towage and insurance, a handsome profit was made on their brief involvement.

2.2 Bristol scrap merchants (WSL) – August 1947 – May 1949

Bennett and Brewis acquired the wreck from the insurers for just £25,000 in August 1947 (£15,000 lent by WMC). None of their records survive so we have only press articles and references on WMC files as source material.

Nothing is known of how the Bristol merchants arrived at their bid of £25,000 for a wreck that could (based on MI initial 1946 costings) produce at least £152,000 of revenue, albeit with great difficulty due to the ship being wrecked. Indeed, increased metal prices led Brewis in 1948 to value the ship's metals at £250,000. The purchase was backed to a very large extent by WMC and their interest was in the valuable non-ferrous metals that the wreck contained. Of course, the Bristol merchants and WMC would have had no access to MI's costings, showing an estimated 1,025 tons of non-ferrous. WMC's agreement with WSL enabled them to buy the non-ferrous from WSL at £40/ton, less than its market value of at least £53.

After commencement of demolition in September 1947, the Bristol merchants removed the funnel, superstructure, and most of the tough nickel chrome steel in the four big 15-inch turrets before encountering severe financial difficulties. Available evidence suggests that 2,000 – 2,500 tons of steel and 250 tons of non-ferrous were extracted by them. Unless WSL had negotiated a special deal with BISCO due to the difficult conditions, the steel would have been sold at the controlled scrap price of between £3.40 and £4. Total income might have been £17,000 given the 250 tons of non-ferrous sold to WMC at the agreed price of £40. Costs in the nine months to July 1948 were said to be £17,000 with the major cost being a weekly payroll of £500. Therefore, an estimate for the 21 months to May 1949 would be upwards of £30,000 costs, generating significant losses.

BRISTOL SCRAP MERCHANTS 1947-49 – ESTIMATED FINANCIALS	
	£
Revenue	
Steel (say 2,000 tons)	7,000
Non-ferrous (250 tons @ £40)	10,000
Total revenue	**17,000**
Costs, say	(30,000)
Estimated losses	**(13,000)**

2.3 WMC – Phase 1 – Bauer as contractors - May 1949 - January 1952

WMC acquired the wreck for around £30,000 in May 1949. Provided the ship could be refloated to facilitate demolition at a more suitable location than Prussia Cove, the ship could still yield at least 21,000 tons of steel and maybe a further 875 tons of non-ferrous material. Potentially a very profitable project if the ship could be moved,

WMC engaged Bauer to salvage and move the ship. Their efforts were entirely focused on patching the hull up for refloating until this was achieved in July 1950. There was no revenue from the sale of scrap in this period as none was extracted. A significant 'up front' investment by WMC.

Bauer's costs were invoiced monthly to WMC, adding 5% to costs as a contribution to their overheads. Bauer surprisingly received no 'success fee' or other reward when the ship was refloated. They were entitled to a profit share, but there was no profit in these early stages. Monthly cost sheets show that unsurprisingly the major expense was wages which peaked at £750/week in November 1949.The tugs that moved the ship to Marazion in July 1950 and then attempted to move her inshore, later in the year, cost a not insignificant £3,750.

Surprisingly even after the ship was moved to more sheltered waters at Marazion in July 1950, no scrap was apparently extracted until early 1951. Much time was instead expended on meetings with local bodies and on further patching up the ship to facilitate moving to an optimum location. Bauer's costs were reduced though and even in 1951 wage bills were only between £200 and £300 weekly. The first significant scrap revenue of £40,661 was generated in the 7-month period to 31 December 1951. 2,518 tons of steel and 15 tons of non-ferrous were extracted. Steel was thankfully sold to BISCO at prices well above the controlled scrap price, reflecting the additional costs of extracting steel from a shipwreck. The agreement with Bauer was modified twice to defer reimbursement of their costs by WMC until scrap recoveries were achieved. Better scrap recoveries enabled a profit of £4,893 to be shared in the 7 months to December 1951, even after paying off £4,582 arrears of Bauer costs. Bauer were no doubt not too happy though at still being owed £4,013 by WMC on 31 December 1951.

WMC had received just 15 tons of their favoured non-ferrous metals and a profit share of £3,000 by the time the Bauer contract ended in January 1952; a paltry return for them on total costs paid out by them of around £165,000. WMC had written off £35,000 of these costs in their 1950 accounts as irrecoverable and hoped for better fortunes in future if the ship was broken up profitably.

In January 1952, WMC chose not to renew their contract with Bauer, partly due to disputes over recharged costs. Accountants for both Bauer and WMC then engaged in acrimonious correspondence on the level of these recharges as well as prices for the sale of plant by Bauer to WMC. Bauer appointed receivers in February 1952, due to insolvency.

WMC – PROFITS AND LOSSES - BAUER CONTRACT MAY 1949 – JANUARY 1952		
Income/(Expenditure)	**£'000**	**Profit/(Loss) £'000**
Scrap revenue	43	
Carriage/Sundries	(7)	
Bauer salvage costs	(32)	
Profit	**4**	
Bauer profit share	(1)	
WMC profit	3	3
WMC balance sheet		
Cost of ship	30	
Bauer accumulated salvage costs	135	
	165	
Written off as irrecoverable – 1950 accounts	(35)	(35)
Salvage costs c/f / (Overall project losses for WMC to January 1952)	**130**	**(32)**

2.4 WMC – Phase 2 – the 'Macs' February 1952 – August 1956

When the venture was completed in 1956, WMC reported variously in the press that they had made overall a profit of £35,000 and £52,000 on the venture. However, no working or calculation of these figures has been traced or reasons for the difference in their reported profit figures. The £52,000 figure is assumed to be more accurate since it was declared later after the project had been completed and all figures known.

WMC informed the financial press that this profit was down to big increases in non-ferrous scrap prices in the period since the ship's acquisition in 1949, although at one time, they were '£120,000 down on the deal'. This represented roughly the accumulated expenditure by WMC on the WARSPITE project at the end of 1951 when little revenue had yet arisen. When the Macs were engaged in early 1952, WMC's managing director told them that the project was '£30,000 down', this represented roughly the write off in WMC's accounts of expenditure thought to be irrecoverable, a different measure.

The Macs turned all this into a reported overall profit for WMC of £52,000 so the period of their management was undoubtedly remunerative for WMC. Neil Macdonald and Neil MacQuarrie (the Macs) had worked for Bauer and were familiar with the challenges faced. As well as their basic wage, they negotiated incentive payments based on the level of metals from the wreck, despatched from Penzance. They also insisted that appropriate plant and equipment was made available. They were hard working managers, working long hours alongside the workforce, whereas Bauer had been London based. The Rolls Royce gas turbines were first deployed in May 1952 to refloat the ship, making it easier to move the hulk around. In May 1953, the ship was cut in two, again making this difficult project a little more straightforward. The project moved along smoothly without the friction that had existed between WMC and Bauer.

The first accounts under the Macs must have been encouraging to WMC, showing operating profits of £29,000 for the 14 months to March 1953; 4,665 tons of steel and 182 tons of non-ferrous being extracted. No precise figures are available for subsequent periods to completion in August 1956, but contemporaneous estimates of future steel outturn suggest total steel out turn was similar to that on WARSPITE's sister ships, see table on next page.

WMC continued to negotiate high prices for steel scrap with BISCO (shown below), well in excess of the controlled steel scrap price, which at the time varied between £6 and £8.50; the special BISCO price falling to £14.50 in 1954 presumably as the ship was reduced in size and became easier to break up closer inshore.

1952/3	£17.00
1954/6	£14.50

Plenty of steel left for salvage in this 1953 or 1954 image of the bow section. The barge **EMPEROR** is alongside being loaded with scrap. *Negus Penzance*

Alloy (nickel chrome) scrap fetched £2/ton more than these carbon scrap prices. Until 1955, BISCO did not expect the steel scrap from WARSPITE to be cut into sizes that could be put straight in the furnaces at the steel mills, as would be normal for other shipbreakers. BISCO would pay £1.75/ton more for furnace sized plates.

For 1952 and early 1953, non-ferrous was sold for £122-£132/ton, significantly more than the £53/ton that MI had anticipated in their 1946 estimates. The prices achieved by WMC for non-ferrous scrap are not known after March 1953 When the demolition had finished, WMC maintained that profits had arisen as non-ferrous prices had increased 'three or four times' since their acquisition of the ship in 1949. Sales of non-ferrous from two aircraft carriers broken up TW Ward in 1955 and 1956 had achieved an average price of £231/ton, which tallies with WMC's 'three- or four-times' statement, assuming similar results were achieved on WARSPITE. Demolition costs are not available after March 1953 although specific items such as the bonuses to the Macs (£15,000) and ex gratia payment to the Bristol scrap merchants (£5,500) are known.

The author has compiled the table on page 89 below from actual figures to March 1953 and reasoned estimates thereafter. One peculiarity is the high proportion of revenue derived from steel scrap (as opposed to non-ferrous) due to the special high prices paid by BISCO. Revenue from steel scrap is calculated by reference to the special BISCO prices and estimated tonnages, similar in total to the actual outturn from two of WARSPITE's sisters, HMS MALAYA and HMS QUEEN ELIZABETH. Assumptions have been made about demolition costs per ton, based on reductions from those incurred in 1951/3 due to the wreck being demolished more efficiently as it was moved closer to shore and cut in half. The reader may find the figures in the table of interest, but they should be treated with a little caution.

Outturns from WARSPITE's sister ships are known and shown below, along with MI's estimate for WARSPITE (Appendix 7) and the estimate for WARSPITE is shown below.

HMS WARSPITE AND SISTER SHIPS – OUTTURN FROM DEMOLITIONS			
	Ferrous	**Non-ferrous**	**Total**
QUEEN ELIZABETH	26,650	1,135	27,785
VALIANT	26,068	1,269	27,337
MALAYA	26,733	1,161	27,894
WARSPITE – MI estimate (appendix 7)	23,675	1,025	24,700
WARSPITE – actual estimated - p84,89	26,783	1,032	27,815
All these ships, except MALAYA, had been the subject of varying degrees of modernisation during the 1930s, possibly affecting their tonnage. WARSPITE actual estimated above included Bristol scrap merchants' results.			

The project, in conclusion, was risky but made some money for WMC; no doubt a big relief for them and their shareholders given the significant 'up front' salvage costs and capital employed in the project. The author will leave the final word to a latter-day shipbreaker.:

The most striking thing is how lucky the companies involved were – the market prices moved up hugely. Despite that luck, they still didn't make a major profit, which shows how absurdly optimistic the whole project was from the start.[37]

Rather a harsh comment perhaps and great credit must go to the workforce on the project in getting the job completed.

[37] Ian Watson, Managing Director, Shipbreaking (Queenborough) Ltd. August 2022.

HMS WARSPITE PROJECT – WMC – ESTIMATED PROFIT AND LOSS ACCOUNT 1949/56				
	May 1949-Jan 1952	**Feb 1952-Mar 1953**	**Apr 1953-Aug 1956 (est)**	**Total**
Scrap tonnage extracted	**Tons**	**Tons**	**Tons**	**Tons**
Non-ferrous	35	182	565	782
Steel etc	2,518	4,665	17,600	24,783
Total	2,553	4,847	18,165	25,565
Prices/ton (£)				
Non-ferrous	£114	£122/£132	£165/£231	
Steel	£12.50/£14.50	£17.50	£17.50/£14.50	
Revenue	**£'000**	**£'000**	**£'000**	**£'000**
Non-ferrous	4	26	116	146
Steel	39	81	272	392
Total	**43**	**107**	**388**	**538**
Expenses				
Carriage	-7	-13		-20
Bauer costs	-32			-32
Direct		-32		-32
Labour		-28		-28
Commission		-5		-5
Est costs			-218	-218
Profit	4	29	170	203
Allocations to				
Bauer	-1			
Macs bonus				-15
Bristol scrap merchants				-5
Deferred costs to Jan .1952 w/o		-20	-110	-130
WMC Profit	**3**	**9**	**40**	**52**

APPENDIX 3 – RESCUE OF WARSPITE CREW BY W & S LIFEBOAT – APRIL 1947

Timeline of a rescue

April 20

WARSPITE leaves Portsmouth.

April 22

0415 am Duty Officer Portsmouth asks nearest lifeboats (Penlee and Lizard) and two tugs to be ready as weather bad. WARSPITE then 20 miles south of Penlee.

c800 am Alert called off as weather has improved.

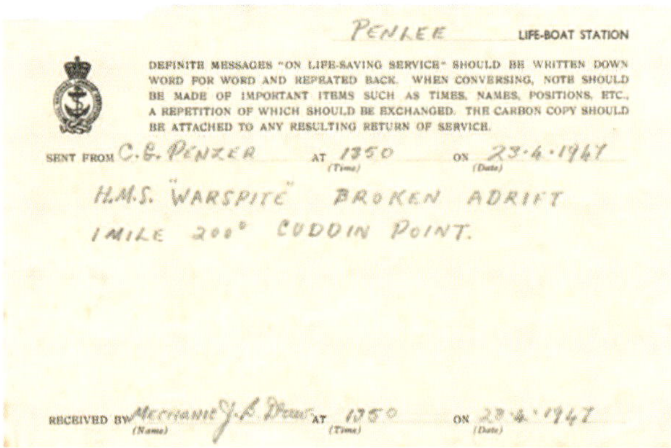

PENLEE LIFE-BOAT STATION

DEFINITE MESSAGES "ON LIFE-SAVING SERVICE" SHOULD BE WRITTEN DOWN WORD FOR WORD AND REPEATED BACK. WHEN CONVERSING, NOTE SHOULD BE MADE OF IMPORTANT ITEMS SUCH AS TIMES, NAMES, POSITIONS, ETC., A REPETITION OF WHICH SHOULD BE EXCHANGED. THE CARBON COPY SHOULD BE ATTACHED TO ANY RESULTING RETURN OF SERVICE.

SENT FROM C. G. PENZER AT 1350 (Time) ON 23·4·1947 (Date)

H.M.S. "WARSPITE" BROKEN ADRIFT

1 MILE 200° CUDDIN POINT.

RECEIVED BY MECHANIC J. B. DREW (Name) AT 1350 (Time) ON 23·4·1947 (Date)

April 23

1350 Coastguard messages Penlee lifeboat to say WARSPITE adrift one mile southwest of Cudden Point.

1400 Penlee lifeboat W & S launched and makes way to WARSPITE.

1545 Lifeboat returns to Newlyn as WARSPITE crew content to stay aboard.

1730 Lifeboat launched for a second time.

1815 Lifeboat reaches Prussia Cove and begins dramatic rescue of crew of WARSPITE.

1945 W & S returns to Newlyn with WARSPITE crew.

There follow two dramatic accounts of the rescue by those who were there and played a major role.

1. Lifeboat motor mechanic Johnny Drew

Perhaps the best account of the heroic rescue of the WARSPITE crew is that of senior mechanic, Johnny Drew[38]. His first-hand memory of his and indeed the boat's greatest achievement follows.

It was around midnight on 22 April 1947 that we were instructed to get all the crew together and stand by for instructions. Informed that the Lizard lifeboat station was on the same errand. We were there in the boathouse for about two hours, waiting till the telephone rang, and said, 'Stand down, as the WARSPITE wasn't in any

[38] This account was transcribed by Graeme Ewens and first published in his book 'Life of a Boat' (Buku Press, 2021).

danger'. So, we stood down and came to our homes. We had a powerful radio receiver at home, and I took the habit of tuning into the shipping, the distress band. When the WARSPITE got into difficulties in our vicinity off the Wolf Rock, I was concerned that I didn't miss a message. I could hear the tugs talking, so I knew first hand that she was adrift and broken from her tugs. The weather forecast put out that it was going to increase to gale force, or even severe gale force, and I don't think I did go to bed that night. I was so involved listening first hand. It then came out around midnight and the early hours of the 23rd that the tugs were going to attempt to tow her to Falmouth Bay. But the weather was so bad, and she was such a huge ship that the tugs couldn't really handle her. They felt, with the force of the weather, it was best to tow her to the nearest possible safety, which was Mount's Bay, around the Lizard into Mount's Bay. They were going to attempt to pull the WARSPITE crabwise, where one tug had a wire on her stern, and another would have a wire on her bow. And going into this gale one tug would go this way, and the other would tow the other way. But she was always going to leeway all the time, so that's what they were doing through the night, because it was getting pretty dramatic. And I thought she's going to go ashore in Mount's Bay. It was night-time now, and they eventually got her into the east side of the Bay off Mullion and Porthleven. The tugs were there, but way offshore, and they dropped anchor in that position between Mullion and Porthleven.

Now the weather was severe gale, and the forecast wasn't improving, it was getting worse. When daylight came the wind didn't alter at all. It was from the southwest and the WARSPITE was on a deadly shore. Now, with the flood tide she had her anchor down, and the strain was so severe. Midway through the morning I went to the lifeboat house. The first thing I do is go on the radio, so I was in touch with all that was happening. I had the engines warmed up because I felt sure we were going to be called. Then I went home, and I was in the midst of having my dinner, up around one o'clock, when one of the crew, second mechanic Jack Wallis, called to our back door and shouted, "Johnny, come on." I said, "What's on?" "WARSPITE's adrift in the Bay."

She had broken from her anchor cable and was being driven towards Malpas Ledge. Everyone on the seafront could see a huge great ship like that. I left, got to the Front. Then right away the coastguards fired the maroons and called out the lifeboat. We ran to the lifeboat station, and we launched about 2 o'clock and proceeded towards her. But the Ledge she was on, Mount Malpas Ledge, there wasn't more than a fathom of water on that Ledge. The surf from the sea was churning up so much that you could almost touch the bottom with the boat's paddle. The crew had shouted at them to come off and they wouldn't, they refused, saying they were safer on the ship than on the lifeboat. The Cox'n said, "Well we can see our life is at risk," because one nasty sea could capsize us. "We are not stopping in this position. If you're not coming off, we are returning to Newlyn."

On returning to Newlyn, there was press and radio reporters wanting news of what was happening. The crew went back to Mousehole around three or four o'clock. As was natural to me, I stayed on the lifeboat. Because in any case I had to refuel again, and I made sure the tanks were full. Because I felt sure we were going to be called out again I sent one or two of the crew to have petrol sent out by car.

I remained there putting everything shipshape again. I was on the verge of coming ashore now, locked everything up, because there was nothing left to do. I was berthed about six boats off the end of the pier, the lifeboat was. After I locked up, I didn't even get to the pier, got to about the second or third boat and I could hear men shouting. There was the lifeboat crew running down over the pier and waving to me to start the engines. So, I ran back and started the engines, had them running. They were all aboard now, casting off and in the harbour, putting on our oilskins and life jackets.

Penlee lifeboat **W & S** on the slipway. *Harry Welby/RNLI Penlee*

When we left the harbour there was a cross sea, which means right on the beam. The sea was southeast and the wind was south sou'west, with a full sea on the starboard beam. As we steamed further along that course, there was a lot of shallow patches all along that coastline. We had to go off at a certain degree of land, and as we were approaching what we call a butting beam on our port beam, you could see the superstructure of the WARSPITE on the cliffs. There she was, and the sea was going over us, terrific sea. The Cox'n went further onto eastward until we get a full vision of the WARSPITE. She was lying right into the sea and the wind, so that gave us no lee, what we call a leeside, to go on for shelter. Every twenty feet you were running into very shallow water. Well, I wouldn't say it was frightening, but I was a little bit scared, because the Cox'n altered course and ran in towards the WARSPITE. As we were getting closer in and could see these terrific seas, bow right down under the water and right up to her steering bridge and all that. The breakers were going up there because she was down by the head. The waves were breaking on the port side but there was a channel of about forty yards between us and the port side of the WARSPITE.

In discussion with the second Cox'n and three or four of us were talking in the cabin, because you couldn't stand on deck. We had to look astern to see the seas that were coming, rolling up, as we call it. If one hit you, you went up. We were aiming for the WARSPITE at full speed, doing eight knots. And as we were running towards her this channel was becoming more clear, the Cox'n decided he thought we would make it. I had everything battened down. "Everything alright boy?" "Everything alright Cox'n." "OK."

We didn't go more than a few yards and the sea was rolling up at the stern of us. Well if it hit us at the speed we were going, I don't know if I would be here now. But the Cox'n saw it coming. He said to me right away, "Ease the engines down." So I eased down to just below half speed. Well, that sea did break, it broke just as it hit the lifeboat. It swept everything, the lifeboat was under water and all our hatches were closed, no water could get below, but it did what we call "swept" her. It rolled in between us and the WARSPITE. All you could see was this breaker rolling in, a great white one rolling into the shore. Now, if we were going at any speed, we would have gone in with that sea. But we slowed down. It hit us and bounced us in. Now you can see the danger? They normally come in threes, big seas like that. We had a couple more of those but, having slowed down that gave the safety of the lifeboat. So, you put to the channel and the Cox'n said, "I think we can make it."

So we're going now, not dead slow, but steering our way on the lifeboat. We went down this channel, nothing but white water, just steerage way. When we got down towards the port quarter of the battleship there under the stern of the lifeboat there was nothing but rocks breaking all around, so near the stern of the lifeboat. If you made a slight error the lifeboat would have touched these rocks and that would have been it. But we were relying on seamanship and entirely on machinery. They were our salvation. When we got under the stern of the ship and brought the lifeboat around, head into the wind and sea, we got the lines onto the ship, one for the bow, one for the quarter. With the wind and the sea coming in, the second Cox'n, the second mechanic and myself we couldn't stand up, so the best thing to do was to kneel under the canopy to be steadier and have better control. Then with the cox'n's orders for 35 minutes it was nothing but, "Full ahead. Full astern." As the breaking sea was coming and hitting the lifeboat, we'd come full astern, then ahead to keep her in position. So we were see-sawing to keep the lifeboat in position. At the same time we were sometimes up level with the deck and sometimes thirty feet down. Each man jumped onto our deck, one at a time, until we took them all off. I know one man did slip and went down between the lifeboat and the ship. But a couple of the good crew members on board soon had him. We saved the eight of them.

Now, when we came down one time, we could hear splinters. As the lifeboat dropped on this occasion, she dropped on the WARSPITE's torpedo blisters. When all big battleships were built, their armour was sometimes a foot thick. Torpedoes would be set at the water line. These torpedo blisters were all the length of the ship, practically just below the water line. They would be projecting out, so if a torpedo hit, that would cushion the blow before it hit the ship. That's the torpedo blister. When we came down on that we heard splinters. We said the lifeboat was damaged somewhere under the water. We cut the ropes clear and we did not come out full ahead. The Cox'n was very cool and collected and said, "Just less than half speed so we can dodge out into the weather."

So we dodged out at that speed until we got well clear of the WARSPITE, out into the open sea again. From then on things improved, not the weather, but as far as our safety was concerned, following the open seaway. Well the Cox'n had control and could head up for Newlyn. We arrived sometime after seven I should think. Newlyn pier was black with people, thousands of them. In the fields watching the lot.

The first thing I did then, I said to the Cox'n that we try all the handpumps in all the compartments to see if that blow we heard in the splinter had damaged her under water. If any of the compartments was damaged it would fill with water. Fortunately there was no water. So we hadn't damaged the hull. A day or two later when the boat was re-housed on the slipway we found what the damage was. It was the handrail which is around the bilge keels of all lifeboats. So if anyone was in the water they could grab it. Two on the port and two on starboard. If anyone wanted to be rescued, he had something to grab onto. While the screeching of the wood we heard on that occasion was one of these handrails damaged, split right off, but the lifeboat hull wasn't damaged and we didn't make no water.

There was a ship's lifeboat slung out on a davit on the WARSPITE's port quarter, so it was exceedingly difficult for the Cox'n to bring the lifeboat into a correct position to be clear of that boat. She was an obstruction regarding the rescue. What he did was, as soon as we got in that position, we had our two masts up and our aerials were set from mast to mast. But so that he could manoeuvre and get in that position, he lowered down the forward mast onto the lifeboat, so that all two thirds of our boat would be clear without any obstruction. So the mast was down while you did the rescue. Well the Cox'n relied on me; he knew it all but just needed reminding that our radio communications were out because the aerials were down. When we were leaving the WARSPITE to come out, there was the lifeboat's recognition to the coastguards and vice versa—coastguards to lifeboat. You had recognition hand signals in practice ever since the lifeboats were built. Hand flares, and you had to memorise them, know them very well. They were your contact from shore to lifeboat before radio was involved. So as soon as we took the crew off, and me knowing we couldn't call up on the radio and give information, I said to the Cox'n, "Put out our hand flares?" "Right," he said. Took out a flare which burns green to white. When we took it out and one of the crew lit it up, it burned a second or two green and then it turns to white. That indicated to them on shore that we had taken off all the crew. Had we shown green and the other was green, that meant we took off part or none. The third one, which we hoped we never used, was red, if we were in trouble. But the green to white was essential. Although we were out of radio contact, we had done the service and were returning. As soon as we got out into the open seaway, I said to the Cox'n, "We ought to send a radio message." "Well," he said, "slow her down." So we slowed her down to put the mast up and set the aerials. I then went down to the cabin and called up Land's End Radio and gave them the final message that we had taken the eight crew off and we were returning to Newlyn.

The assistant mechanic was Jack Wallis. We had a pretty good understanding. He was very thorough, very thorough. He was a good seaman as well. When the Cox'n said, "Full ahead," it was full speed. We opened our two main throttles to full. The two throttles were open and the engines were running to their full governors. When we came ahead, it was full ahead; when we came full astern, it was full astern. It was instant; it had to be. That's why the service under those conditions proved so successful."

2. Transcript of 1957 BBC Radio programme on the rescue

The story below is initially relayed by Captain Baxter, captain of WARSPITE on her last voyage...and then by Kerr, the BBC presenter, Chambers, the coastguard and Eddie Madron, coxswain of the lifeboat. It looks at the rescue principally from WARSPITE's viewpoint, making a good contrast to Drew's account.

Baxter: We got somewhere off the Lizard – that would be early afternoon of the 21st. The weather was quite bad then, it wasn't atrocious weather at that point but it was starting to blow up fresh and unfortunately the tug BUSTLER which was the big horsepower tug, our main tug, she parted her line. And I got in touch with the tug on the Aldis lamp and they said they would try and reconnect the next morning. Meanwhile the METINDA held us up to the wind all that night. Daylight the next morning, the BUSTLER attempted to reconnect up forward on the starboard bow, but it was quite impossible. Well, he got down to the after end on the starboard side and tried and tried. Oh, we tried for several hours to connect, but of course the wind was very bad by this time. The WARSPITE was jumping about and the tug was jumping about a lot more than the WARSPITE was – being much smaller. I and he just couldn't connect at all. And eventually in the early afternoon, we did manage to connect by means of his coming very close indeed, in fact so close that he might well have knocked some plates or rails off. However, he didn't do much damage and we got connected up. Unfortunately, we were in the position then of having METINDA on the port bow and the BUSTLER on the starboard quarter, this isn't a very good towing arrangement because when one was pulling one way, one was pulling the other and so it was very, very difficult to manoeuvre the vessel at all. However, it was the only place the BUSTLER could get connected and I suppose it was better than nothing. Now it appeared that the BUSTLER and METINDA could at that stage not actually manage the craft because the weather was too bad. By that time of course it had reached practically gale proportions and we eventually got into Mount's Bay.

Now Mount's Bay is not much good as an anchorage in a southerly gale. As a matter of fact, it's a recommended anchorage for a northerly gale. It's into leeward, and you just get no shelter whatsoever. But the weather was very bad; the tugs couldn't stand it any longer and around about 11 o'clock at night the tug BUSTLER flashed me a message to say we should prepare to anchor because they couldn't hold us any longer. So, we got the anchor more or less ready for letting go and on the word from BUSTLER we let go the anchor and the ship swung round and laid to her anchor, reasonably comfortably at that point. However, at daylight in the morning the wind undoubtedly freshened. And it blew an absolute whole gale, wind eight, force eight – something like that.

And it would then be about south south-west I should think, and it was apparent that the vessel was dragging her anchor and dragging it very quickly.

Kerr: Because of the storm, coastguards were on bad weather watch and at first light on the 23rd of April, coastguard Chambers took up his watch in a small lookout hut high on Cudden Point near Prussia Cove.

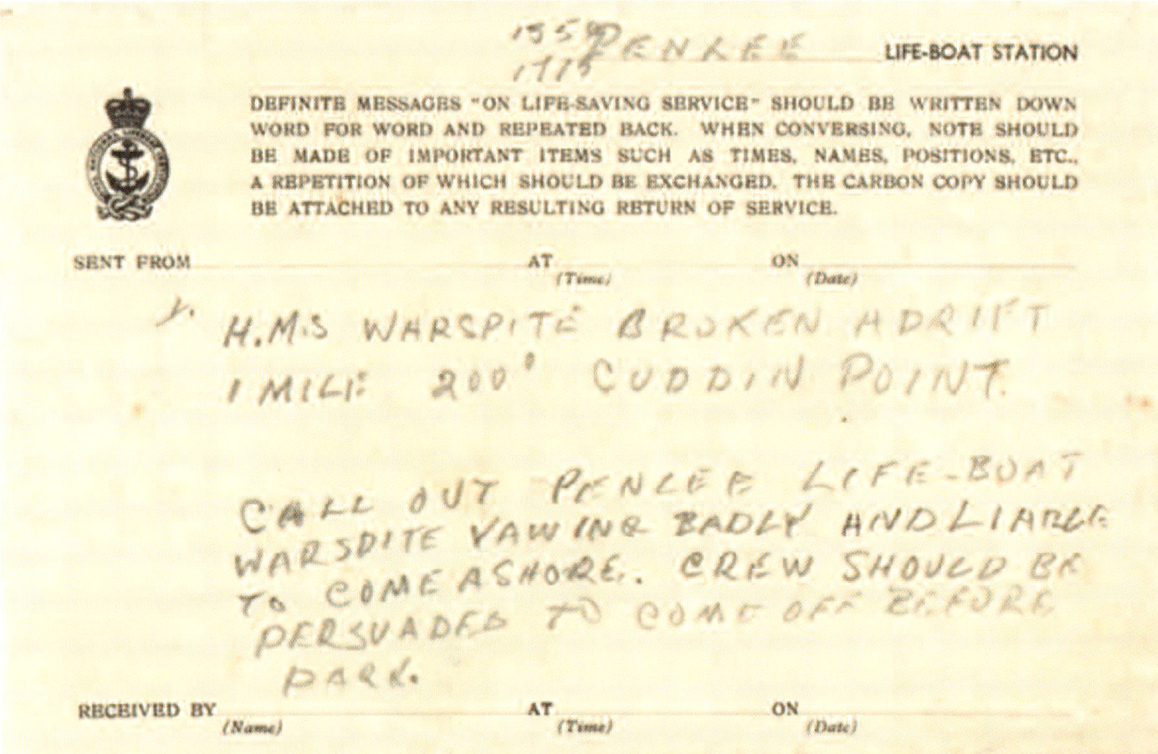

1550
1119 PENLEE LIFE-BOAT STATION

DEFINITE MESSAGES "ON LIFE-SAVING SERVICE" SHOULD BE WRITTEN DOWN WORD FOR WORD AND REPEATED BACK. WHEN CONVERSING, NOTE SHOULD BE MADE OF IMPORTANT ITEMS SUCH AS TIMES, NAMES, POSITIONS, ETC., A REPETITION OF WHICH SHOULD BE EXCHANGED. THE CARBON COPY SHOULD BE ATTACHED TO ANY RESULTING RETURN OF SERVICE.

SENT FROM AT (Time) ON (Date)

H.M.S WARSPITE BROKEN ADRIFT 1 MILE 200° CUDDIN POINT.

CALL OUT PENLEE LIFE-BOAT WARSPITE YAWING BADLY AND LIABLE TO COME ASHORE. CREW SHOULD BE PERSUADED TO COME OFF BEFORE DARK.

RECEIVED BY (Name) AT (Time) ON (Date)

Johny Drew collection, courtesy of Elaine Bawden

Chambers: Well as soon as I went on watch, the usual thing for a Coastguard to do if there's any ships anchored is to take in conjunction with the Coastguard station on his flank, he takes a bearing especially if there's signs of rough weather coming on, which I did when the WARSPITE was there. But that time she was about 1½ miles from Cudden Point, southwest of Cudden Point. After taking the cross bearing about 8 o'clock I took another bearing myself and I didn't realise that she was on the move in a north-westerly direction with the tide. The tide was coming up to flood, that's high water. As soon as I saw she was adrift I got on the phone but unluckily the phone was out of order and I ran down to my opposite number, Mr Dunn, and told him by any means he could to contact Penzer Point to get in touch with the Hon. Secretary of the Penlee lifeboat and have the lifeboat launched. Well, Mr Dunn, he grabbed the first car he came to, and he went down to Marazion post office and done the necessary.

Kerr: While the call for the lifeboat was being passed, the WARSPITE was moving closer inshore. Just before midday she struck on a reef 1¼ miles from the shore. At noon the lifeboat was launched from its station on the opposite side of the bay and for the Coxswain, Edwin Madron, this was an important call. Though he had served as a lifeboatman for 30 years this was his first mission in command. He was to need all his experience.

Madron e knew very well that she was dragging very fast then and she was in trouble. Terrible sea running, so we went under the inside the ledge and went to her starboard quarter. I asked the skipper whether his crew would be taken off in the breeches buoy and they refused. The skipper thought they were safer on WARSPITE than they would've been on the lifeboat. So, I told him then we should have to return to the station in case of any other calls, we couldn't remain there.

Kerr: Captain Baxter had asked his crew if they wanted to leave in the lifeboat. They all felt as he did that the WARSPITE was not yet in a hopeless position.

Baxter: Well of course we didn't want to leave at that time because the ship was in a reasonably safe position, as safe as you can be in weather like that, and I told the Coxswain of the lifeboat that I thought we should stay where we were as we appeared fairly safe. He pointed out that when the tide made, we'd probably drift over the top of this mountainous reef and carry on dragging and eventually strand on the rocks. Well, it transpired just exactly as he said. As we got very near the reef under Prussia Cove there and then the anchor appeared to hold, it stepped straight out from the bow and leading towards where the anchor had evidently got caught on something on the bottom. However, the strain of the WARSPITE so high out of the water and such a strong wind blowing – indeed such a gale blowing – the strain was too much for the cable; the cable parted, the ship swung broadside round and got picked up and dashed onto the rocks under Prussia Cove. Unfortunately for our old cook, he was all right – he wasn't that old in fact – he was only a lad actually, but it was his first trip at sea and he was in the galley after great urging to make some tea and see if he can produce something warm to eat as we were feeling a bit cold by then and when she struck she healed over to port and her bow went a little ways under the water and she took about 7 or 8° list and the cook, his pots and pans and part of his galley stove and everything went flying down to the low side of the Galley and he came out very fast indeed. I decided that would be the end of that – we wouldn't have anything more to eat that day.

Madron: We came back and within a quarter of an hour, well I never had any chance to have a cup of tea poured out and didn't have a chancc to drink it before the lifeboat was wanted again for the WARSPITE she's gone ashore into old Prussia Cove. Well, when we arrived at Cudden Point, I seen the position of the WARSPITE and it was practically useless to attempt anything on her starboard side as it was all broken water and about 100 feet from her port bow there was another ridge so we needed all the speed we could, so we use no drogue sail and got inside the reef.

Kerr: Madron's next problem was how to approach the ship and get the men away. The WARSPITE lay, headed outward, within 100 yards of the granite cliffs and with the rocks close under her. Seas reckoned to be 30 feet high were breaking against her bow and sweeping along both her sides. They passed along her to bounce against the cliff and sweep back again and meet other incoming waves, causing dangerous broken water.

Madron: One minute the lifeboat would be down with the WARSPITE's propeller right in line with the boat and the next minute we'll be looking right in at the quarter deck. You'd almost think that the lifeboat would be thrown right in on the quarter deck at times. After a few minutes there was the heady ground sea would strike the bow of the WARSPITE so we would go full ahead on both engines and, just before it broke on the lifeboat stem, we'd come full astern otherwise the back surf coming down over the starboard side would take her right up on the bilgeways. In about five and twenty minutes with both engines going from full ahead to full astern we worked her along on the port quarter just clear of the port propellers which was very dangerous to the boat and eventually the crew all jumped in the lifeboat.

Kerr: Getting away from the WARSPITE and into open water was as great a problem as the rescue itself. The lifeboat, tossed high and flung about, had to pass clear of the rocks and fight into the storm. Madron managed this. It was all a magnificent piece of courage and seamanship and was to be acclaimed the outstanding rescue of the year. Coxswain Madron was decorated with the Lifeboat Institute silver medal for gallantry, his senior mechanic received the bronze medal, and each member of the lifeboat crew was awarded a testimonial in vellum.

Captain Baxter shakes hands with Eddie Madron and his crew on 'This is your Life' 1957.
Edwina Reynolds Collection

W & S – Subsequent history 1947- 2023

The W & S continued to serve at Penlee until 1960 when she was replaced by the ill-fated SOLOMON BROWNE, tragically lost with all hands on 19 December 1981. W & S served as a reserve RNLI boat until 1970 when she was sold to the first of a series of private owners. By 2013, she was in poor condition when acquired by Captain Rod Shaw MBE who has done a tremendous job in restoring her, despite vandalism in 2020 and a freak wave in 2022 causing setbacks. The full story of the W & S lifeboat is recounted in the excellent 'The Life of a Boat' by Graeme Ewens (Buku Press – 2021).

Views of **W & S.** Above: Largely restored in August 2017. Below left: Tragically vandalised in September 2020, causing over £5,000 of damage. Below right: After being sunk by a freak wave at Harwich, March 2022. *R. Shaw*

APPENDIX 4 – NEWSREEL FILMS OF WARSPITE IN CORNWALL

4.1 Introduction

Seven newsreel films have been traced on YouTube, a word search for the titles shown below should trace them for playing. None are long but the images are interesting and reveal how the breakup and salvage is going. Where there is commentary, it is often stirring!

4.2 'WARSPITE and SAMTAMPA wrecks', British Pathe (1947, 89 seconds)

The steamship SAMTAMPA was wrecked the same day as WARSPITE, 23 April 1947 in the Bristol Channel. 39 of her crew died, along with 8 from the Mumbles lifeboat. An awful tragedy. This is a silent film with some clear aerial images, about half the film for each ship.

4.3 'HMS WARSPITE goes aground in heavy gales', Gaumont British News (1947, 61 seconds)

Aerial view with stirring commentary

4.4 'HMS WARSPITE aground' (1947, 57 seconds)

Silent film taken from a boat approaching the stern of WARSPITE, very clear view. The funnel and most of the 'tower block' bridge has gone so later than the stated date of 1947.

4.5 WARSPITE to be refloated, Movietone News (1950, 54 seconds)

Evocative images and commentary of the ship at Prussia Cove and workers going back and forth on the breeches buoy. Some of the bridge is left on the ship. Images of the pumps and a fleeting glimpse of St Michaels Mount at the end, meaning film must have been completed 1950 or later.

4.6 'WARSPITE', British Pathe (1950, 117 seconds)

Taken at Marazion, a DUKW is pictured taking works from Marazion beach out to WARSPITE and clambering up a rope ladder aboard. The wooden decking is virtually gone. The bow is dry but the quarter deck is awash with water. A small ship with a tall funnel, BARNET, is alongside. We are told the wardroom is being used as a workshop.

4.7 'WARSPITE moves on', British Movietone (1950, 43 seconds)

The tow from Prussia Cove to Marazion.

4.8 HMS WARSPITE, Marazion, Mount's Bay, Cornwall, Eagle Photographic (1950, 182 seconds)

Evocative but not at all top-quality film. WARSPITE under tow from Prussia Cove to Marazion. Storms breaking over her at Marazion. Made from two 16mm film reels found quite recently. Some pictures of personnel who might be identified in due course.

APPENDIX 5 - CITATIONS FOR MEDALS – GALLANTRY IN MARCH 1950 EPISODE

Awarded the George Medal.

Thomas Convery, Foreman Rigger (Ardglass)
James Craig, Shipwright Diver (Aberdeen)
Neil Macdonald, Principal Salvage Officer (Stornoway, Isle of Lewis)
Neil MacQuarrie, Assistant Salvage Officer (Oban)

Awarded the British Empire medal (Civil Division)

Herbert Bullen, Shipwright Diver (Stromness, Orkney)
Peter Hynes, Welder (Kilsyth)

(All of P. Bauer (Salvage) Ltd)

While salvage work was being carried out on the vessel "WARSPITE", three salvage hands entered the air lock entrance to a section which was under pressure and then went into the compartment below. They found the compartment to be in good order and after about 20 minutes they began the ascent of the ladder back to the airlock. Whilst climbing the ladder two of the men were overcome by gas but the third man managed to reach the deck and gave the alarm. As soon as he learned what happened MacQuarrie accompanied by Convery, entered the pressure chamber and without hesitation, descended the ladder to the unconscious salvage hands. The two rescuers were soon affected by the noxious gas which produced a heaviness in the limbs accompanied by a dazed condition. Nevertheless, MacQuarrie and Convery made every effort to get one of the men up the ladder to the airlock but they became weaker and had to abandon their task. While Convery remained in the pressure chamber, MacQuarrie returned to the deck for help. Taking a rope with him he re-entered the airlock with an assistant who lowered the rope to Convery while MacQuarrie descended the ladder, but Convery lost consciousness as he tried to tie the rope around one of the unconscious men. MacQuarrie then attempted to fasten the rope but he too lost consciousness before it could be secured.

Macdonald who had been engaged ashore, returned to the ship at this stage and took charge of the rescue work. He first gave orders for a gentle flow of oxygen to be fed into the pressure chamber and then entered the airlock with Craig. Together they descended to the pressure chamber and raised Convery to the airlock where he was taken out on to the deck in a state of delirium and semi-consciousness. Macdonald and Craig immediately returned to the airlock and were joined by Hynes. Macdonald again descended into the pressure chamber but was now becoming exhausted and could not raise MacQuarrie but after further efforts fastened a rope to the unconscious man who was then hoisted up to the airlock by

Craig and Hynes. Macdonald saw that Craig was losing consciousness and helped him back to the deck. Meanwhile Hynes had been joined by Bullen and they entered the pressure chamber and were successful in raising one of the unconscious men with the aid of a rope.

Craig had now recovered and undeterred by his previous experiences, entered the pressure chamber for the third time and helped to complete the rescue.

(Supplement to the London Gazette 5 June 1951)

APPENDIX 6 – SOME PEOPLE INVOLVED IN THE WARSPITE PROJECT

Research has ascertained quite a bit of background data on people mentioned in the account above. Normally this is from their families. We start with the 'two Macs', who played such an important role in the WARSPITE project and then in 1957 founded the successful MacSalvors business.

6.1 Neil MacQuarrie (1927-2020)

Neil was born in Tobermory, Isle of Mull. Three of his uncles were captains in the Mercantile Marine; two of whom were decorated for bravery in saving their ships in wartime. One successfully brought his crippled ship to port when carrying a cargo of high explosives, after being torpedoed amidships. The other uncle was decorated for manoeuvring his ship whilst under heavy bombardment during the evacuation of Crete.

Neil was originally going to join the police force as a cadet but he changed direction and became a salvage diver, ultimately with the Bauer organization. One of the first operations he participated in was on the NEVADA II off Coll and then the BREDA, which had sunk in Oban harbour in December 1940 with a valuable cargo of aircraft spares and tyres. He was first a diver's tender for Jim Craig (see 6.7) and learned to dive on the BREDA. Soon after this time he got to know Neil Macdonald (see 6.2) who came from the Isle of Lewis. All three were later to work together on the WARSPITE.

From June 1945 to December 1946, Neil worked for Bauer's Le Havre office in clearing Mulberry harbours and the wrecks of the 'Gooseberry 2' ships sunk to create breakwaters off Utah and Omaha beaches for the D Day landings. He particularly focused on the old battleship HMS CENTURION and the KENTUCKIAN and EXFORD.

He was also involved with wrecks sunk in the river Seine at Rouen and in associated cofferdam work. Here he met fellow divers Ken Holden and Donahue Caskie, both also from Mull.

CENTURION sunk as a gooseberry.
I. MacQuarrie collection

A reference from Bauer at that time spoke highly of him as a skilled underwater worker and diver as well as being diligent and serious, expert in the use of the Cox bolt gun, oxyhydrogen underwater cutting equipment, explosives, and patching work. Neil was also involved on other salvage jobs such as a torpedoed grain ship in Wales and the tanker LUNULA, torpedoed in 1941 in the Thames. In 1949, Philip Bauer chartered an aeroplane in France and took Neil over the wreck of the WARSPITE. Shortly after this, Bauer started work as a contractor for WMC, and so Neil joined the workforce around July 1949. He was initially employed as the ship's diver.

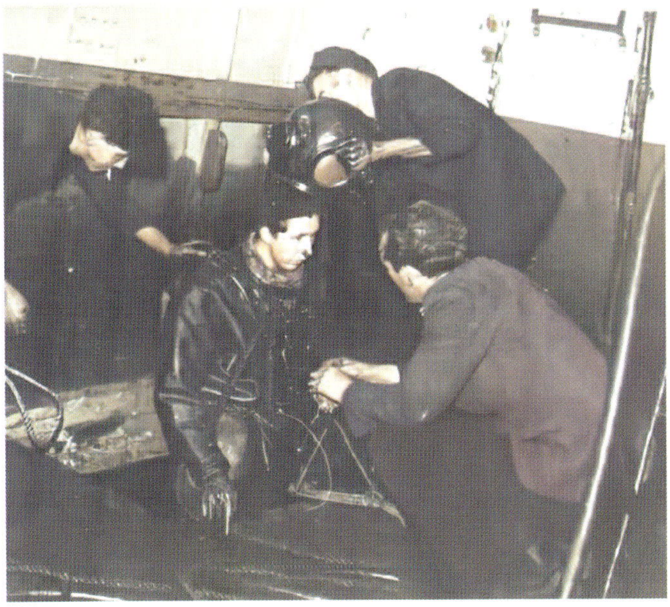

Neil MacQuarrie as a diver on WARSPITE, emerging from fuel tank.
I. MacQuarrie collection

If he had not got involved with WARSPITE, Neil had plans to work on wreck clearance and associated activities in Haifa and Trincomalee. He was a director of the Port Clearance Authority around this time, a body responsible for wreck clearance in Haifa.

In 1950, John Lennie, Neil's older brother, who was previously in the Mercantile Marine, died in an accident on the WARSPITE after working on the ship for just two months (see chapter 3 above), a tragedy compounded by the death of Neil's younger brother just 5 weeks earlier at the age of 16 after a short illness.

In February 1952 Neil was the salvage officer on the sunken collier SALTFLEET on the River Ouse. From early 1952 the Macs successfully took over the day-to-day control of the operations with Frank Wilson on WARSPITE, occasionally working on other jobs such as the stranding of the King Harry Ferry whilst being towed from Falmouth Docks and early salvage on the LIBERTY which ran aground at Pendeen in 1952.

When the WARSPITE work ended he and Neil Macdonald formed the MacSalvors partnership in 1957 which was to endure until the death of Neil Macdonald in 1996. The MacSalvors business continues to this day.

6.2 Neil Macdonald (1921-1996)

From the Isle of Lewis, Neil was educated at the Nicolson Institute in Stornoway. He joined the Merchant Navy in May 1944 where he became a salvage engineer on board the RANGER at Uig, Isle of Skye – OHMS HT Salvage (Hired Transport Salvage). He was then engaged at Rothesay and Milford Haven until June 1945. In 1945 whilst on board the salvage vessel RANGER, Neil was awarded the Testimonial on Vellum from the Royal Humane Society. A fellow member of the ship's crew had fallen into the water and Neil jumped in to save him. In 1945 he joined the BAFFIN in Milford Haven where he met Neil MacQuarrie and then worked while based on board the BAFFIN until 1947 in France before starting work on WARSPITE.

The Two Macs on BAFFIN on which they worked off Normandy.
K. Macdonald collection

Neil worked on WARSPITE throughout a large part of her time in Cornwall. From late 1949 he is described as 'senior salvage engineer' and when Bauer took over in 1949, he became the highest paid employee, earning £15 a week. He was widely respected:

"Big Neil knows what he's doing, they say and talk of the giant Scotsman with

the quiet voice who knows his job inside out. Neil Macdonald is the engineer in charge of the refloating attempt and there are few people around Penzance and Germoe who don't know something about him."[39]

Neil attended meetings in that capacity, with, for example, the Newlyn harbour commissioners in September 1950. This was to discuss the beaching of the WARSPITE after she was refloated. He also negotiated for the purchase of plant, equipment, and supplies. During these years he was also engaged on other activities for Bauer.

One item once deployed on the WARSPITE project: The P&H crane in MacSalvors 'colours', lifting the new Porthleven fishing boat **SADIE WYKEHAM** for transportation to the World Fishing Exhibition in 1963 or 1965. *N.C. MacQuarrie collection*

In February 1951, for example he was to undertake salvage work on the tanker ATLANTIC DUCHESS in Swansea Docks badly damaged by explosions and fires.

In April 1951 with divers Craig and Pullen from the WARSPITE team, he participated in salvage work on ships in the inner harbour in Haifa, Israel, using a floating crane, notably the PATRIA, sunk by Jewish paramilitaries in 1940. Later that year the Macs worked together on the RAMSES II at Sharpness, living on board for the duration of the operation even though she listed at a precarious angle.

After the ending of the Bauer contract in January 1952, he, and Neil MacQuarrie, the 'two Macs', with Frank Wilson successfully managed work on WARSPITE for WMC until the project finished in 1956. They then formed the successful MacSalvors business shortly afterwards in 1957 and MacSalvors Crane Hire in 1962, this in part used equipment, previously used on the WARSPITE project.

---

[39] Cornishman 22 June 1950.

6.3 Bill Brewer (1926-)

Bill is believed to be the last survivor of the team working on the salvage and demolition of WARSPITE. His role was to drive a DUKW out to the wreck taking out between 40 and 60 men out every day for an 8am start on the wreck in Mount Bay. He did this for around three years and left before the wreck had been demolished. (He was not involved at Prussia Cove.) Other duties included carrying a photographer out to the wreck (WMC arranged photos every four months) and in the latter stages taking a mechanic out in the evening to pump out the stern section (after the ship had been cut in two and there was just one deck left to cut up), so it was fit for working the next morning. On one such evening occasion in 1953 or 1954, Bill met a Chief Petty Officer in full uniform on the walkway around the stern. Bill and the CPO smiled at each other and then the CPO disappeared. Bill was in shock and believed he must have seen a ghost. The next morning, Bill was grilled by manager Frank Wilson and the Macs about his "sighting", but his story was taken seriously. It was thought the CPO may have been killed in action off Crete, although the basis for this is unclear.

When the ship was well cut down, Bill recalled that hundreds of wooden boxes with spares for the ship, were found. He has retained some brass plates from these and some 'day logbooks' retrieved from the wreck. He remembers what was left of the boilers being blown up, but only after extremely valuable 'white metal' had been extracted. Earlier, he had spotted in the demolition that, due to wartime action, two boilers had been damaged (but not repaired) and close by there were numerous 4-inch concrete blocks, which had to be blown up. Bill still has one of these, pictured in chapter 7 above. Although never actually on the beach he remembers that the bow section stood well out of the water at low tide. From time to time a barge visited (probably EMPEROR) and took scrap off the wreck and into Penzance for loading on to railway trucks. Once the barge broke down and Bill got the DUKW to tow the barge, a much bigger vessel, into Penzance. Another time the DUKW's petrol was contaminated so it broke down and Bill and the two Macs were stranded on the Hogus Rocks awaiting rescue for three hours. Bill talked also about early attempts to extract metal and how wash basins had been smashed to facilitate the removal of taps as scrap. Bill is clearly proud of his involvement with WARSPITE.

6.4 Brian Tunstall-Behrens (1885-1968)

Brian Tunstall-Behrens was educated at Marlborough College and Pembroke College, Oxford. He was 27 when he commissioned and oversaw the building of Porth-en-Alls, Prussia Cove, managing all the craftsmen, ordering the materials, and settling the accounts alongside the architect Philip Tilden. The house is the first visible example of reinforced concrete being used in a domestic context and is probably one of the earliest examples of its use in the west of England. His engineering ability (a Captain in the Royal Engineers during the 1914/8 war) underpinned this pioneering technique and the local craftsmen took some convincing that such long unsupported and loadbearing spans were possible.

The arrival of the WARSPITE on the morning of 23 April 1947 was something of a disaster for Brian Behrens and his family. There was a very real possibility that the wreck might never be removed but break up over many years, very probably leaving evidence on the beaches to this day. Utterly dominating the coves, it changed the atmosphere of the place completely – possibly forever – and put hitherto unknown peaceful Prussia Cove on the national map. To this day, people in their 80s revisit the place saying they first went there to see the WARSPITE. Meanwhile the rush of tourists to the site, many reaching Prussia Cove by car even in 1947, caused the approach lanes to be impassable and a surge of visitors short-cutting across agricultural land. It was a very tense moment and at one point and in desperation to turn the situation to advantage, it was suggested the ship be turned into a restaurant! The fisherman gave up fishing and made an easier living taking tours around the wreck, their canny wives setting up cream tea cafes where tackle had been stored.

Sea View and The Haven were soon let to the Bristol scrap merchants (initial owners of the wreck) to accommodate an office and labourers, but this was hardly compensation and as it turned out, even these agreements ended in somewhat bitter and protracted correspondence as the condition of the two houses on the eventual departure of the tenants was truly shocking. There was a nearly catastrophic fire and it seems the furniture and even some fixtures and fittings were removed and sold! It took months to restore the houses to a habitable state after some three years of brutal occupation. An earlier letter highlighted issues:

On the 8th November last I wrote direct to your subsidiary company at Sea View in which I drew particularly their attention to the choking of the gullies with food (that should've been scraped off the plates before washing) washed down the sinks. The consequent overflow over the ground augmented by the bath water soaking into the foundations at Sea View and running down the road in front of the house and causing a nuisance to my tenant lower down,
... the offal from the canteen lies around the back doors uncovered and drawing rats and vermin. It only requires someone to draw the attention of the Inspector to the state of this and both of you and I shall be involved in expense and trouble.[40]

[40] Letter of 14 January 1950 from Brian Tunstall-Behrens to WMC.

Given that Sea View had been the destination of many early family holidays when it was a guest house in the 1880s and later the family's home in Cornwall, it must have been especially upsetting to see it damaged in any way by the salvage company. Aside from building Porth-en-Alls house in 1912, the family's intention has always been to preserve Prussia Cove which has remained virtually unchanged since. The WARSPITE was certainly a great threat to that intention.

P. Tunstall-Behrens collection

Brian Behrens was half German, and this background was enhanced by his being a master at Gordonstoun under the headmastership of Kurt Hahn. His Germanic attention to detail might explain the pedantic correspondence with his departing tenants, but the gift from them of a gunmetal ashtray though gratefully received, rather than acting as a souvenir of happy days, may have perpetuated a bad memory!

A note by a grandson, Peter Tunstall-Behrens, current owner of the Porth-En-Alls estate.

6.5 Duncan Nicholson (1920-2018)

Duncan was the engineer on the project from 1947 to late 1953 or thereabouts. He devised the breeches buoy (or Blondin wire) out to the ship and in late 1951 he commented candidly to WMC on what he saw as the poor performance of the contractors Bauer. He must have been roused as one of his nieces referred to Duncan as being "a very quiet person, didn't like fuss".

The following account of his life was written by his son David in March 2022.

Duncan was born in Dennis Road, Padstow on 18 July 1920, the last but one of six children born to Duncan Taylor Nicholson II, an electrical engineer and Georgina, a musician. Duncan's father ran a small power plant in Padstow and installed electric street lighting in the town. He later installed the ice works and was a member of the Padstow Masonic Lodge. Duncan was educated at Padstow and Bodmin schools, later completing an engineering apprenticeship at J. Stone and Company in Deptford, London. Some of the work he was involved in included building the watertight doors and propellers for the QUEEN MARY. On completion of his apprenticeship, Duncan joined the Ellerman & Bucknall Shipping Lines as a junior engineer, sailing the East Africa route. As World War II progressed, he joined the Atlantic convoys, and sometime later his vessel was attacked and sunk, either by torpedo or dive bombing.

This left Duncan severely traumatised (possibly post-traumatic stress disorder) and later needing admission to a psychiatric hospital for treatment. He was then discharged into the care of his older brother, Ralph and moved down to West Cornwall to be close to their older sisters. When he recovered, Duncan opened a small garage at Praa Sands and although work came in, sadly payment didn't, either being delayed or not paid at all! So, when work on the WARSPITE became available, he and Ralph both joined up and Duncan became the Chief Plant Engineer. Duncan also made two trips to Scotland to bring down the tug boats needed for the work. On one trip (possibly later) while towing a barge, they encountered a storm and the barge was lost as the towing hook was pulled straight, such was the strain on it.

D. Nicholson

On the WARSPITE, Father became friends with Ted Heather (the uncle of a school friend of mine) whom he remained in contact with until Ted's death. Ted at that time, lived in a house overlooking Pixie's Cove, so didn't have far to go to work. My father was very much a "now" person and never really spoke about his time on the Atlantic Convoys, and only little snippets of information about working on the WARSPITE, which I shall recount here. One favourite tale of Father's was that he found a queue of men, trying to get into one of the gun turrets. The guns had been removed but the optics remained, and the men were taking turns observing a couple on the cliffs nearby, who were engaging in some very personal matters. Apparently, the sights were of such good quality, everything could be seen. Getting back to the WARSPITE, when the bolt on armour plating was removed, it was cut up using thermic lances that required much oxygen. The large tanks of oxygen were carried by a man who had been nicknamed as 'Hopalong' (which he hated) as he had either only one leg or it was deformed in some way (I met his son some years ago in a Penzance pub, which is how I found out about his father's dislike of his nickname). The large amounts of compressed air needed in the re-floating was supplied by taking it from the compressor section of three or four Rolls Royce jet engines they had on deck. Father went to Rolls Royce to undertake a course on the engines. I'm afraid I don't know much more.

After working on the WARSPITE, Father went to work with the Iraq Petroleum Company on the oil pumping stations based in the Iraq desert (I was born in Kirkuk, which was very different to my two older brothers who were born in Penzance!) ending up as Chief Mechanical Engineer (pipeline). After a brief time in neighbouring Iran, he returned to the UK around 1973 and worked for Cornwall Farmers, then worked as a technician at Mount's Bay School in Penzance before retiring. Father then devoted a lot of his time model making, his masterpiece being a nine-foot-long model of the S. S. Great Britain with a working engine and for which he won many prizes. At 85, Father was still exhibiting his models and also rebuilt the kitchen at home among other things. He began to slow down at 90 and died aged 98 in the early hours of 27 November 2018 in a nursing home near Camborne, having suffered from Alzheimer's for a few years. The family still has a lamp from the WARSPITE captain's cabin, which was a fixture in the family home. He was an all-round engineer, who could turn his hand to anything – mechanical, electrical, or wooden. One of my brothers and I carry on this tradition.

The ashes of Duncan and his wife are scattered near the post at Prussia Cove from where his Blondin wire went out to the ship, as this was where the couple originally met.

6.6 Joe Barnes (1917-2013)

Joe Barnes worked as an estimator at WMC, ascertaining the extent of recoverable materials. He is pictured below in an image received from his daughter Janet Wilce. Janet wrote about him in March 2022.

The youngest of 2 sons and completely self-taught. He couldn't go to school because he was a sickly child and the family could only afford one pair of shoes and so Dennis, the oldest brother had those and went to school. He had a heart problem and wasn't expected to reach his teens but as you see he lived to a ripe old age. He volunteered for the 2nd World War but at the recruiting office they asked how he had got there, and he told them "On the bus". They provided transport home to his mother as they told him he wouldn't survive a return journey on the bus. So, he remained working at WMC and was a volunteer fire officer. He always told the tale about when Coventry was being bombed, his was the only engine which had a bell (found in the scrap metal). The engine took a direct hit, but the bell survived rolling and clanging down the street. Part of my dad's job was to go and tender for purchase of items for salvage. Sometimes it was only parts of vessels. I remember him pondering how he could just tender for cabling on a submarine but in this case, it was the whole vessel. I haven't got much left, he donated most of the "stuff" to a maritime museum in Cornwall, but I can't remember which one. I suspect it might have been around Marazion. I did go there once and it was a small harbour. (Note by author – believed to be Charlestown). I know my dad was concerned about all of the teak a lot of which was just burnt. Things were so different then. All the

pews in Tettenhall Church were made out of the teak and my dad who was into wood working made me a bedroom suite out of it when I was first married. The only thing that I have left is a blanket chest and a nest of tables which came from his house.

An interesting fact which I remember, well at least I think it is interesting, which may not link directly with WARSPITE is about the many miles of cabling in ships. For some time, it was considered waste as the metal content was encased in so much rubber material and it was too labour intensive to make it viable. My dad found a way of stripping this and using the rubber mixture. The rubber was chopped finely for want of a better term and sold to stables for schooling horses in the winter months. It was the forerunner of the materials used now. I don't know definitely but it was probably about 1949. As a young girl I can only remember him always going to dockyards. WARSPITE was by far the most well-known at least as far as I know. There was talk about submarines, but I don't recall any by name, I am fairly sure that they would have been from Plymouth and that would have been mid-50s. I remember being on holiday and being told to look at the rusting vessels all tied up there. When they had worked out about the stripping of cabling there was a lot of GPO phone lines that came along but can't remember much about that. WMC was the only place he worked. He started as a messenger boy and was still there when it became part of IMI.

6.7 Jim Craig

Jim was a skilled worker who worked on various jobs around the country as a salvage diver. He was a shipwright diver from Aberdeen. In the 1930s he worked on the salvage of the German High Seas Fleet at Scapa Flow with Cox and Danks. He was able to turn his hand to all tasks underwater and this is why the Macs wanted their fellow Scot on the WARSPITE project. He was awarded the George Medal for his gallantry in the March 1950 accident and was instrumental in cutting the great ship in half in April 1953. After WARSPITE, he is understood to have worked on Holman's dock in Penzance.

6.8 Jack Hawthorne

Jack (John) Hawthorne joined the workforce as an engineer in 1950. When the project was over, he became the maintenance engineer for the Moorlands Sheepskin factory at Pool; one of the largest local employers at that time.

APPENDIX 7 – METAL INDUSTRIES: TRANSCRIPT OF THEIR APRIL 1946 ESTIMATE FOR DEMOLITION

General. The only official data so far available to us is that contained in Jane's Fighting Ships, prior to the vessel's modernisation. The present displacement of the vessel is not yet available to us, but we understand that the WARSPITE now has a normal displacement of 30,600 tons, maximum displacement 35,000 tons.

As built. The WARSPITE was constructed at Devonport between 1912 and 1915 and then had a displacement of 31,000 tons normal and 33,000 tons maximum. Her length was 600 feet between perpendiculars, overall, 643 feet, beam 104 feet, maximum draft 33½ feet mean draft 30⅔ feet. She carried 8 - 15-inch guns and 12 - 6-inch guns with minor armament.

Rebuilding, the ship was reconstructed to some extent between 1925 and 1933 including the remodelling of the control top and bridgework, addition of bulges and the doubling of the anti-aircraft armament. In 1935 the WARSPITE had further reconstruction of an extensive character. In particular the turbines were replaced by four smallish, geared turbines and the boilers were replaced with 24 '10 ton' water tube Yarrow boilers. The 12 6-inch guns carried have been reduced in number to 8 and extra armour protection has been fitted on her decks.

We estimate that in her maximum displacement would be included the following:

Ammunition	2,600 tons
Fuel oil	3,400 tons
Water in Boilers, Feed and drinking water tanks etc	1,000 tons
Stores	1,550 tons
Crew and Effects	150 tons
Total	**8,700 tons**

This would leave an actual weight of the vessel itself as 26,300 tons, a figure which could no doubt be checked on reference to the Admiralty. Of this figure we consider that 4% could be reckoned as wastage in the form of cement, paint, rust, fire bricks, composition, tiling etc., and 2% could be allowed for actual cutting losses, leaving a probable actual outturn of 24,700 tons.

Distribution of weights

We estimate these are as follows:

Distribution of weights		
Hull	38%	10,000 tons; includes non-ferrous 2%-200 tons
Guns, turrets, magazines, torpedo tubes, etc.	15%	4,000 tons; include non-ferrous 10%=400 tons
Armour and protection	25%	6,500 tons
Machinery, including boiler rooms, engine rooms, shafting, propellors, etc.	13.5%	3,500 tons; includes non-ferrous 15%-525 tons
Wood and general outfit	8.5%	2,300 tons
Total		**26,300 tons; includes non-ferrous 1,125 tons**

The main armour on this ship is stated to be Krupps cemented and varies from 13 inches to 6 inches and 4 inches at the ends. There is heavy armour around barbettes, gun houses and funnel uptakes.

10-inch armour plate unbolted from WARSPITE for scrap and cut in half to facilitate transportation to shore. *Walsall*

In addition, it is believed that she has a longitudinal bulkhead, port and starboard, covering the machinery spaces which is understood to be of a nickel alloy. The deck armour, before modernisation was chiefly HT. We do not know what the new deck armour put on after modernisation is made of.

The market for nickel chrome scrap is rather uncertain at the moment.

Detailed estimate and probable values

We would make the actual outturn as follows:

	Tons	**Price per ton (£)**	**Total value £**
Steel scrap	12,240	3.40	41,510
Nickel chrome and other scrap alloy	6,000	5	30,000
HT quality armour	2,000	3.40	6,800
Gun scrap	1,200	3.40	4,080
Cast iron	500	4.40	2,200
Boiler tubes	400	16	6,400
Shafting	110	12	1,320
Non-ferrous	1,025	53	54,325
Lead and zinc	100	30	3,000
Anchors and cable	75	20	1,500
Sundry fittings	500	4	2,000
Teak	150	9	1,350
Firewood, etc.	400	0.50	2000
Total outturn	**24,700**		**154,685**
Deduct breaking costs, say £2 per ton			**(49,400)**
Net outturn			***105,285***

Note 1 - It is highly probable that the Admiralty will have stripped the ship quite considerably before handing it over. The extent of that stripping will only be confirmed by actual inspection.

Note 2 – compare HMS THUNDERER

Normal displacement 22,500 tons, length between perpendiculars 545 feet, length overall 581 feet, beam 88 feet.

Outturn	**Tons**
Scrap steel	9,511
Nickel chrome	5,430
Nickel steel	1,058
Gun scrap	615
Gun wire	92
Cast iron	449
Boiler tubes	156
Cables and chain	32
Sundries	125
Teak	160
Non-ferrous	786
Lead and zinc	79
Total	**18,493**

Source: MTSC – File 12059/4.

Metal Industries estimate – author's comments.

The breakers understood total weight of the ship was around 35,000 tons when fully loaded. However, 8,700 tons of this would be ammunition, fuel, stores, and crew etc so metal would be 26,300 tons. Of this, 1,125 tons would be the more valuable non-ferrous metals. However, 4% of the total would be materials that could not be recycled and 2% lost when the oxy-acetylene torches were used to cut. There are limited outturn statistics for the actual demolition of HMS WARSPITE in Cornwall, but appendix 2 above endeavours to estimate these.

APPENDIX 8 – VESSELS INVOLVED, 1947-1956

The following is a selection of vessels, identified as supporting in the WARSPITE project.

Ship	Type	Year built/ GRT	Role	Notes
BUSTLER	Tug	1942/1100	Lead tug for tow to Faslane April 1947. Chartered by MI from Admiralty	Sold to Yugoslav interests 1973, renamed MOCNI then SMJELI 1989
METINDA III	Tug	1945/593	Tug for tow to Faslane April 1947.	Ex-EMPIRE JEAN. Bought by MI for £40,000 in 1946 from Admiralty.
W & S	Lifeboat	1930/	Rescued WARSPITE crew, 23 April 1947	Still afloat and under restoration at Harwich.
CHEW MAGNA	Pinnace	1944/21	Salvage work, towed scrap barges.	Originally owned by Bristol scrap merchants.

GLEBE, a vessel similar to **CHEW MAGNA**, pictured at Tollesbury in 1990. *Phil Simons*

EMPEROR being towed into Penzance by a DUKW with a cargo of WARSPITE scrap.
Negus Penzance

Ship	Type	Year built/ GRT	Role	Notes
BARNET	Tug	/379	Salvage duties. Features on film noted in appendix 4.6.	Beached Penzance 1951 or broken up c1952.
DISPERSER	Salvage	1912/287	Acquired by Bauer Sept 1946. Possibly salvaged by Bauer at Kirkwall 1944	Broken up in 1953 or earlier.
EMPEROR	Cargo	1906/97	Three trips a week carrying ship scrap to Penzance. Built as sailing boat, ketch.	Scuttled in 1956 as in poor condition.
RADNOR	Barge		Carried ship scrap	
FREEBOOTER	Tug	1940/762	Stood by 5 July 1950 for first attempt at re-floating.	Scrapped Genoa, Italy 1959.

Admiralty tug **FREEBOOTER** in 1947. *WSPL*

Ship	Type	Year built/ GRT	Role	Notes
ENGLISHMAN	Tug	1944/762	Towed refloated hulk 29 July 1950 and 12 October 1950.	Ex-HM tug ENCHANTER, renamed CINTRA 1962
BRAHMAN	Tug	1938/230	Towed hulk 29 July 1950.	Ex-HM Tug EMPIRE LARCH. Sold to T.H. Piggott Grimsby and renamed LADY VERA. Converted to motor ship 1963. Sold 1969 to W.E. White and Sons and renamed LASH WHITE. Sold 1973 to Thames Services and renamed TURBULENT. Arrived Bruges for demolition 1974.
MASTERMAN	Tug	1941/482	Towed hulk 29 July 1950 and 10 November 1950.	Sold 1962 to Yugoslav interests and renamed SMJELI. Broken up Split 1971/3.
SEAMAN	Tug	1924/369	Towed hulk 12 October 1950.	Broken up Queenborough by Lacmots Ltd 1964.
TRADESMAN	Tug	1944/593	Towed hulk 12 October 1950 and 10 November 1950.	Ex-HM tug EMPIRE JULIA. Broken up 1973 in Turkey.

United Towing tug **SEAMAN** assisting **PORT NICHOLSON** in Hull. *Ken Guyatt/WSPL*

APPENDIX 9 – HMS WARSPITE – A BRIEF ACCOUNT OF HER SERVICE CAREER

Many excellent books have been written on this great ship and this note can only be a short summary as this book is about her last nine years in Cornwall. When completed in 1915, WARSPITE and her four sisters were probably the most powerful naval ships in the world. They broke new ground in being oil rather than coal fired as well as having newly designed 15-inch guns – these could fire shells 55% heavier than their German equivalents. Armour was up to 13 inches thick. They were 644 feet long. Appendix 6 has more detailed information on WARSPITE's size and specifications.

HMS WARSPITE launched at Devonport 26 November 1913. *Author's collection*

As part of the 5th Battle Squadron, WARSPITE played an important and dramatic role in the biggest naval battle of the First World War, Jutland in May 1916. Her steering gear jammed, causing her to steam in almost two complete circles, dangerously close to the German fleet and being hit by heavy shells many times. Steering was to prove an issue at times during her career. World War 1 was otherwise a relatively quiet one for the ship.

WARSPITE was modernised between November 1924 and April 1926 with in particular her funnels trunked, the fitting of torpedo bulges and forward superstructure remodelled – 'WARSPITE 2'.

Seen entering Grand Harbour, Malta during 1938. *WSPL*

A much more substantial programme of improvements took place again at Portsmouth dockyard between March 1934 and March 1937, emerging as an almost new ship at a cost of £2.4m. The bridge structure was rebuilt, and her propulsion system changed, such that similar power could be achieved with 1,500 tons or so less weight. This enabled the addition of 1,100 tons of armour, necessary to counter new heavier plunging shells. Numerous other improvements included better anti-aircraft defences.

HMS WARSPITE leaving Portsmouth for sea trials following completion of her reconstruction in 1937. *Topfoto*

WARSPITE was the most decorated Royal Navy ship of all time and thirteen of her battle honours were won in the Second World War. In April 1940, for example, she led British forces up a fjord in the Second Battle of Narvik and finished off eight German destroyers. In March 1941, she was part of the British forces which sank several heavy Italian units at Matapan. Shortly afterwards in May and June 1941, she was damaged by air attack in the Mediterranean, and this led to a visit to Bremerton yard in the USA until December 1941 for repair and updating. After a period in the Indian Ocean, she was back in the Mediterranean again. However, while providing gunfire support off the Salerno beaches in September 1943, she was hit by a 3,000 lb, guided Fritz FX1400 bomb, arguably the first battleship to be hit by a guided missile. There was also a near miss from a second 'Fritz' and these caused extensive damage; it is said a double decker bus could have driven through the hole in the ship's bottom! Number 4 boiler room was completely wrecked and not repaired as noted by WMC when they came to this, when breaking up the ship. The hole was repaired with concrete after the ship has been towed with some difficulty to Malta and then Gibraltar.

In June 1944, WARSPITE was one of the heavy units on D Day, providing gunfire support to troops landing on Sword beach. Two of her 15-inch guns were out of action though from earlier damage.

Later that month, she was heavily damaged by a German mine off Harwich. She was placed in reserve and given her age and extent of battle damage; it was unsurprising that she was the first of the Royal Navy's operational battleships to be sold for scrap.

Her career made her a renowned and popular ship. The Daily Mail in 1944 exclaimed 'There is a saying in the Navy that wherever there is fighting to be done, the WARSPITE will surely be in it.'

Long may memories of this great ship last!

APPENDIX 10 - FATE OF THE BOATS ON BOARD WARSPITE

Small boats historian Tony Holtham has researched meticulously the history of the boats on board WARSPITE throughout her career. Tony is a leading light in the Small Craft Group of the World Ship Society.

After any ship is built, the composition of the boats on board will change for numerous reasons – these would include refits, damage, enemy action, accidental loss, modernization, change of command or base port, as well as decommissioning, prior to disposal. Boats carried come under three categories, they are either, steam powered, motor powered or pulling/sailing boats. Each category has their own numbering system.

WARSPITE had four davits for lowering pulling craft. The craft initially in these positions were most likely to be a 42ft Sailing Launch, a 32ft Cutter, 27ft Whaler and a 30ft Gig. In addition, stowed in board would have been two 50ft Steam Pinnaces and two 45ft Steam Pinnaces – one fitted as an Admiral's Barge, and the 42ft Sailing Cutter, which may have had the 30ft Gig nestled inside.[41] These were all removed and new boats were shipped on completion of the refit in 1937, and indeed subsequently on several occasions.

On her final voyage to Faslane, a 27-foot whaler was fitted on board and as noted in appendix 3, inhibited the rescue of the crew on 23 April 1947 by the W & S lifeboat.

Below are set out Tony Holtham's notes on the six boats he has traced as having been removed from WARSPITE in her final days after she last saw action at Walcheren in November 1944. The extant records are often patchy, and references are those given by Tony and fellow members of the Small Craft Group to Ministry of Defence documents. The dates of their removal from WARSPITE are not always clear as will be seen.

45ft Motor Launch (MF10413/36) 3698

45' x 11'11" x 2'. 9 tons. Fitted with Kitchener Rudder assembly and a Norris, Henry & Gardner's Ltd diesel engine. Ordered on 9 March 1936 as one of a batch of two 3698-3699 and built in Portsmouth Dockyard as per D1425/36 instructions. On 24 June 1936 was allocated to WARSPITE (MF10413/36 refers) and delivered to WARSPITE on 14 June 1937. Was landed from the battleship at Portsmouth on 20 September 1945. Confirmed then in service at Portsmouth from 15 December 1945 through to 31 July 1957. However, was then surveyed and found to be BER (beyond economic repair) (MAT9307/56 refers). On 21 December 1957 was sold for £21 to Wake Bros Ltd, 9A/B Prospect Road, Mile End, Portsmouth, (CP61672/57 refers).

30ft Fast Type Motor Boat (MF18501/36) 36149

30' x 8' x 1' 7". 3.3 tons. Birmal petrol engines, electrics supplied by Marr. Ordered on 21 October 1936 as per contract CP22070/36 as one of a batch of two from

[41] R Watton – Anatomy of the ship – the battleship HMS WARSPITE *(Conway Maritime Press – 1986).*

Groves & Guttridge, East Cowes. Order confirmed on 19 January 1937. On 24 November 1936 was allocated to WARSPITE (D12440/36 refers). Fitted out as an Admiral's barge as per contract CP38096/36 dated 14 December 1936. Delivered to Portsmouth on 24 August 1937. Transferred to HMS ST ANGELO on 23 November 1939 for use by the Chief of Staff Mediterranean as barge, (MF29382/39 refers). On 13 February 1941, confirmed on board WARSPITE. On 3 June 1941 confirmed with HMS ST ANGELO. On 15 August 1941 confirmed on board HMS RESOURCE (D13949/41 refers) and again on-board RESOURCE on 29 August 1941. Confirmed onboard WARSPITE on 2 July 1946. The craft's whereabouts was queried in PR6588/49. No returns were submitted. Included in AFO 1011/52. Again, no returns were submitted and therefore approval was given to be written off charge, (PR6897/52 and SMBA 4040 refers).

45ft Motor Picket Boat (P3441/42) 42456
45' x 11' x 2'5". 9 tons. Gardner 6LW diesel engine. 13.5 knots. Ordered on 21 February 1942 as per contract CP22756/42 from Kris Cruisers (1934) Ltd Riverside Yard, Ferry Road, Isleworth. On 5 September 1943, the boat was dispatched to the SNSO at Chatham Dockyard and arrived there on the same as per contract CP98827/43. Confirmed at Chatham Dockyard on 8 September 1943. On 16 March 1944 was allocated to WARSPITE, (PO3016/44 refers). At Portsmouth on 20 September 1945 (PO15627/45 refers). Confirmed at Portsmouth Dockyard from 17 December 1945 through to 30 July 1956, when surveyed and declared beyond economic repair as per MAT 7361/57. On 15 March 1957 was brought to produce (BTP), (MAT6269/58 refers).

35ft Motor Boat (P6592/42) 42510
35' x 8'7" x 5'5". 12,900lbs. Fitted with a US Navy model No 4830 6-cylinder diesel engine built by Bude Eng. Co. 9.66 knots. Vessel built by Puget Sound NY as per D2656/42 on 24 January 1942. Yard number 12759. Supplied with spare engine number 4831. On the 24 January 1942 supplied from the US Navy during the refit of WARSPITE by B.A.R.M. at Bremerton Shipyard. On 14 March 1947 confirmed at Portsmouth Dockyard, (P1872/47 refers). Handed over to F Watts at Fareham on 25 March 1948 for care and maintenance, (D7469/48 refers). Confirmed at agents on 24 June 1948. (P3916/48 refers).

35ft Aircraft Tender (P6640/42) 42513
35' x 9'1" x 1'10". 4.75 tons. Perkins P6 diesel engine 17-19 knots. Ordered on the 10 April 1942 as per contract CP35906/42 in batch 42512 – 42517 from J. S. White & Co Ltd Cowes. On 6 September 1943 was allocated to HMS IMPLACABLE (PO10670/43 refers). Dispatched to the SNSO at Portsmouth Dockyard on 28 September 1943. On 7 March 1944 allocated to WARSPITE (D06256/44 refers). On 21 March 1944 was dispatched by road to Rosyth. On 29 December 1944 was ordered to be landed and returned to Portsmouth Dockyard, (D028423/44 refers).

Confirmed at Portsmouth Dockyard on the 17 April 1945. Selected to be converted into a Fast Motor Boat (FMB) for service at Hong Kong, (D8879/51 refers). On 17 January 1952 shipped to Hong Kong for Ships Reserve. On 29 March 1952, confirmed at Hong Kong, (D7944/52 refers) and on 17 June 1954 confirmed still in Ships Reserve at Hong Kong. On 15 June 1955 working for the Captain of the Dockyard at Hong Kong, (PR4849/55 refers). On 13 July 1955 again in Ships Reserve at Hong Kong, (D15390/55 refers). Continued to serve at Hong Kong for the Captain of the Dockyard 7 January 1956, (PR368/56 refers). In 1961 was reported to have been sold locally at Hong Kong, (DM6187/61 refers).

45ft Medium Speed Picket Boat (P18612/43) 43911

45' x 10'6" x 2'4". 8.5 tons. Gardner 6LW diesel engine 13.5 knots. Ordered on the 6.10.43 as per contract CP101928/43 in batch 43911 – 43924 from Thornycroft, Hampton Launch Works, Smith Square, London, (P16038/45 refers). On the 27 October 1944 was completed. Confirmed at Chatham Dockyard on the 18 December 19.44. On the 29 December 1944 was allocated to WARSPITE, (D)28423/44 refers). On the 18 January 1945 was dispatched by MOWT. On the 20 September 1945 confirmed at Portsmouth Dockyard and again on the 17 December 1945. On 10 October 1949 was prepared for issue to HMS HAWKE for use as SCF training, (D25177/49 refers) On and confirmed in service with HMS HAWKE on 30 June 1950. Transferred to Britannia Royal Naval College Dartmouth and confirmed at Dartmouth on 26 May and 3 June 1955. On 17 September 1968 a survey revealed the craft needed a major overhaul. On 12 March 1969 transfer of control was submitted to Dartmouth (DM2499/68 refers. Whilst serving at Dartmouth was given the local identification of PB3. In 1971 was due to be replaced by new construction 45ft MSPBs. It should also be noted that the 43911 as per BR 1315 was sponsored by the Port Auxiliary Service at Devonport in 1962, at Dartmouth from 1964 through to not being listed in 1982.

Abbreviations used above.

BER = Beyond Economical Repair. It means that the vessel may still be of commercial value and to be considered for disposal by the Director of Small Craft Disposals (DSCD).

BTP = Brought to Produce. It means the vessel is considered beyond BER and all items to be stripped prior to the vessel being burnt. However, it has been known for a yard holding such vessels in Care & Maintenance (C&M) to not destroy them completely but to utilise them to repair other craft in order for them to be sold on privately.

APPENDIX 11 - THE RMS QUEEN ELIZABETH EPISODE APRIL 1947

The departure of WARSPITE to Faslane was delayed as her tugs BUSTLER and METINDA III were diverted to assist the RMS QUEEN ELIZABETH which had grounded on Brambles Bank, in the Solent on 17 April 1947. It was reported that BUSTLER later received £15,000 salvage monies.

METINDA III (foreground) and **BUSTLER** (immediately to right of stern of **QUEEN ELIZABETH**). The other tugs' identity uncertain but believed to include **VOLATILE** (two funnel paddler), **RESOLVE** (two funnel screw) and **GRAPPLER** (single funnel paddler). Possibly taken 18 April, 1947.

MTSC (acknowledgements to Paul Brown for support on caption)

THE WARSPITE TEAM PICTURED IN JULY 1950

The WARSPITE project could not have been completed without the support of a great team of hard-working employees. Some were local men and others came particularly from Scotland and Humberside. Those pictured include key players, Duncan Nicholson (front row, left), Neil MacQuarrie (next row, 4th from left) and Neil Macdonald (6th from left) while diver Jim Craig is second from the right in the back row. Also pictured in the 'Macs row' from left are 'Dave', Jack Hawthorne and 'Fred the cook'. In the next row back from left are Ted Heather (2nd), Tom Convery (3rd), 'Jack' (4th), Sunny Pascoe (5th), William Kelly. Not all the team are pictured.

K Macdonald collection

METAL INDUSTRIES YARD - FASLANE

WARSPITE's ultimate destination was meant to be MI's yard at Faslane, built during World War 2 as an emergency military port. She would have arrived in tow, as did her sister **MALAYA** on 12 May 1948 (see top image) and be quickly cut down deck by deck like the battleship **IRON DUKE** which preceded her at Faslane, arriving on 19 August 1946, and pictured perhaps a couple of months later.
MTSC

INDEX OF SHIP NAMES

INDEX OF PEOPLE

INDEX OF PLACES

Back cover top: The **WARSPITE** firmly ashore in Prussia Cove. *MTSC*
Back cover bottom: **BRAHMAN** leads the **WARSPITE** across Mount's Bay. *Penlee*